D0530460

ABOUT THE AUTHOR

Judith was born in Wales but has lived in seven other countries including the Middle and Far East. She is the mother of three grown-up children.

She has been involved in ministry with women for over forty years and has a special interest in the cultures of the Far and Middle East, she has written, lectured and presented on the role of women in these areas.

She is married and lives with her husband, Ron, in Windsor, Berkshire.

SWANSEA LIBRARIES

6000146797

Collar to Cleavage

The Emotional and Spiritual Journey
of an Exotic Welsh Life

Judith Thomas

WITHDRAWN

Copyright © 2012 Judith Thomas

The moral right of the author has been asserted.

Apart from any fair dealing for the purposes of research or private study,
or criticism or review, as permitted under the Copyright, Designs and Patents
Act 1988, this publication may only be reproduced, stored or transmitted, in
any form or by any means, with the prior permission in writing of the
publishers, or in the case of reprographic reproduction in accordance with
the terms of licences issued by the Copyright Licensing Agency. Enquiries
concerning reproduction outside those terms should be sent to the publishers.

Matador
9 Priory Business Park,
Wistow Road, Kibworth Beauchamp,
Leicestershire. LE8 0RX
Tel: (+44) 116 279 2299
Fax: (+44) 116 279 2277
Email: books@troubador.co.uk
Web: www.troubador.co.uk/matador

ISBN 978 1780883 021

British Library Cataloguing in Publication Data.
A catalogue record for this book is available from the British Library.

Typeset in 12pt Bembo by Troubador Publishing Ltd, Leicester, UK
Printed and bound in the UK by TJ International, Padstow, Cornwall

Matador is an imprint of Troubador Publishing Ltd

MIX
Paper from
responsible sources
FSC® C013056

To Ron
Alison, Jessica and Owen
With my deepest love

CONTENTS

FOREWORD

This book can be read for sheer fun, it is a description of one woman's life, lived in many countries, and lived through its joys and sorrows. You can ignore or skip over the questions and thoughts at the end of each Chapter.

★★★

It can also be used at a deeper level, either individually, or as part of a group; making use of the points and question sections in the book. They may be used for discussions of the emotional or spiritual issues raised, or as part of a personal retreat, or just to spend a quiet moment reflecting.

★★★

Some of Life's Lessons Learned – Enjoy!

PREFACE

I am an editor.

I do not mean that profession of being in a publishing house, although I once worked for Cambridge University Press.

I mean that I have *edited* my life. In some parts I have put in the definite, absolute, unchangeable full stops. I have drawn the large, black line, under a marriage of thirty-two years. I have put the question marks after the issues of a tested faith, I have opened and closed chapters with different alphabets – as I have survived – and indeed developed, in the different countries in which I have lived.

Is this now, that classic phrase, 'the full unexpurgated version'? I smile at such an epithet as one for whom, 'doing cleavage' has been a late discovery. 'Collar to Cleavage' – was not an easy move, of which I will have more to say later.

My thirty plus journals spanning three decades, crammed into my shrine of a cupboard, have been freed.

The shorthand code, the illegible writing, the poring of one's soul 'for the author's eyes only', has finally made it into as honest an account of this exotically Welsh life that I can now write.

Chapter One

DEVELOPING WELSH

"Exotically Welsh" is how my daughter describes herself. I like that phrase. I have spent the main part of my life outside the principality, lived in eight countries and have visited over seventy more. All those years of meticulously saving National Geographics are at last rewarded.

How can I, who have spent seventeen years in the States, still say 'lov-er-ly' as if I had just come down from the mountains to water the sheep? How come, when visiting the Welsh community in Patagonia, I am faced with the fact that they can speak Welsh (God's own language) and I can't!

It is a life full of incongruities. I am Welsh, one hundred per cent, blessed with a 'Land of the Rising Sun', Japanese daughter named Alison, followed by two other 'Gemkins', Jessica, born in San Francisco, and a son, Owen, born in New Zealand. None of the three have ever lived in Britain!

How many like Alison have been dressed faithfully in Welsh costume on March 1st – St. David's Day, the patron saint of Wales? What, if I had called her something like 'Angharad Bronwen Thomas'? That would have sparked some interest on graduation day when my beautiful Tokyo Rose walked down the steps to receive her diploma.

Alison, the eight-day-old Japanese citizen, a diplomatic precedent who came into my life with a day's notice, adopted in Tokyo against all odds, by a British couple.

My life has certainly not been dull.

Three children; one with black hair, one blonde, – and a flaming Titian redhead. All born in different countries – to the one they termed, 'psycho-mum!'

Here I am, a woman of a certain 'Simone de Beauvoir' age. Sixty – going on sixteen. One who has finally discovered real love? Somewhere in the past I must have turned over two pages!

Something major was missing. I have now morphed from being a full time priest in the good old C of E, transmuted to being an energized 'suspender wearing – risqué, lingerie-donning, freed troglodyte.' Now I am a "Collar to Cleavage" - wife of Ron.

I have gone from being an industrial chaplain in a chicken factory in New Zealand, ministering on a wing and a prayer, to one who now cooks these feathered friends in a meal for my Action Man. Hollywood could not have written it better.

From a life of academia – interspersed – with many 'Oh Worship the Project' corporate entertaining nights, to ideas of "Where shall we go next?"

I have gone 'sporty' and have learned to kayak. I, who had never swum in the sea – because I feared my feet would not touch the bottom, have now abandoned all reason and plunged into the wild blue yonder – to snorkel in the Red Sea, to flap my flippers in Hawaii!

I now spend Tuesday afternoons having swimming lessons for the over sixties!!

I write that I have gone from a *'from'* to a *'to'* situation, but it is more than that. I have been 'metaphysically morphed,' but more so. It is 'incorporation' in the fullest sense of the word.

My spirituality has deepened, broadened, my ministry extended. Retired, but with a license renewed to embrace all that this new found life offers.

Now I am able and have time to write, to use my experiences and those of others, to write and lecture and give seminars for women.

The seminars have titles like "How to Swim in the Goldfish Bowl of Life without Drowning" and others more close to my heart, "Fit For Purpose" and "Nourishing the Spirit in Today's Crazy World."

Why write? I could not do otherwise. "You should write a book". I have heard it said to me so many times over the years. It bothered me, it nagged at me. The time was right. Whether I was holding on to the rail of an airport bus, or whether I was pouring out my life – in interminable company happy hours, mingling and mangling, I have heard that mantra "Write."

How and where do I begin?

What arrogance has caused me to think that anyone in their right mind would want to read or indeed hear, about such an oddball life?

The sheer conceit of it all.

★★★

Having four degree diplomas on my wall, three in Theology, and having spent an eternity with a first husband who, if I had dropped dead on the floor, would have stepped over me and carried on without a blink, these events have signified to me that my life has not been dull!

My previous attempts at writing were the 'without pain' version, the 'dry' version, without the emotion and the wet pillow of crying oneself to sleep.

It had little to say to the hundreds of women that I have met, those who have brought their stories *to speech*, those who have shared their journeys with me on ground, so holy, that I wanted to take off my shoes.

Writing it all down before, was writing the book that should never leave the store, this time it's different.

QUESTIONS:

The author speaks of a 'metamorphosis.' She writes of a 'from' and 'to' change.

What have been the times in your life when you have felt you have become a different person?

Were there any major situations that marked this change?

What life lessons would you say you had finally discovered?

Chapter Two

THE BOOK INSIDE

I have heard it said that everyone has a book inside them. People share their stories with me, stories to make your hair curl, stories to make your guts turn over, stories of degradation, stories of joys beyond measure, stories of the ordinariness, stories of the routine of love and life, I have heard them all.

In and out of ministry, they have been the mild and abrasive stories which have brightened my soul. Sparkled and surged my spirit.

To be with some thirty people at the time of their deaths, to be a hospital chaplain – as I was at Robert Wood Johnson Hospital, New Brunswick – confronts the great universal truths, we are mortal and life is so very short, fragile.

'Seize the day' has been writ large on my forehead. Like that Everest woman climber, I prefer the 'live one day as a tiger, than a thousand days as a sheep.' How do we seize life with both hands?

Here I sit looking out on a tributary, (a bit of a canal really in Oxford). I sit and write this chapter. The room looks as if it is a minor gallery of the British Museum.

The rug on the floor – bought in Aceh Province, Indonesia, from a bankrupt sea captain who, in turn, had brought it from Iran in the days when you could.

Here is a plethora of Japanese art and china. There is crystal from Prague when it was in the Eastern Bloc. There is a jungle blow-pipe above a book case and numerous baskets from Jakarta that I cannot bear to throw out.

I cannot bear to discard the memories.

In a gesture, which for me was second only to the feeling of abandoning a child, I have this week taken twenty boxes of my books to a bookshop and received nearly four hundred pounds 'Judas money' – that I shall use to visit the three chicks from my nest, who now live in the U.S.

I have, in that wonderful word 'downsized my life' but expanded wonderfully, enlarged my spirit and gone from 'Collar to Cleavage.'

QUESTIONS:

Do you feel, like the author, that you have a book inside you to be written?

If so, what kind of book would it be? What would be some of the chapter headings?

In what ways do your surroundings remind you of your past journey?

The author writes of 'downsizing her life'. How would you cope with 'downsizing' your life at this moment in time?

Chapter Three

STARTING TO REFLECT

Life is so very funny, poignant and cruel – and all the adjectives we have yet to discover. It is far easier to consider and direct others, than to follow that dictum 'know thyself.' I have spent years being interviewed by committees, endless writings of autobiographies and the interminable, putting on paper, my life objectives.

I have had to answer repeatedly, the soul baring question, 'What are your weaknesses?' – As if interviewing panels really cared. My longing was to respond with 'eating chocolate and fantasizing over Harrison Ford' – these could hardly be suppressed!

'What are your earliest memories?' It is amazing that in life, those events which we experience early-on, bring us back later – still in the spiral – but at a higher level.

My father was a trained carpenter and the carpenter's shop was where, from an early age, I wanted to spend my time. The longing was to be a girl carpenter, long before Equal Opportunity Rights was a *p.c.* term. I had my own little carpentry set and would carefully cut out the outline of a parrot on balsa wood. A distorted, raggedy – edged parrot, which would then be painted and a lead weight placed at the end of his tail.

It was perpetual motion on a perch. It was creative, I had produced something unique.

It was in the carpenter shop that I also polished the coffins, the pitch lined coffins, for extra pocket money.

My brother, who was later to go into the business with my father, hated this side of the business.

He abhorred the laying out. Ironically, I would be the one who would lay out my Father after his death.

It was a happy childhood. Martyn, my only sibling, was an adored brother, ten years older. He would take me, his eight-year-old sister to the cinema. This was a relationship that only existed, when he was between girlfriends.

In recent movies I have seen, the plot goes something like this – 'Girl falls for Man, with child tagging along' – the child, is inevitably the sibling or niece – or the offspring of a dead friend, to whom he has made a life-promise. The plot continues – 'Seeing the child, the Girl is attracted to the Man's feminine side. Girl marries man.'

I am not sure this was the case with my sister-in-law, of now fifty years marriage. Was seeing me in tow, a clinching factor in her decision to marry Martyn? I like to think so. This trio existence was not without its unscripted moments.

"Go on, check on Martyn and Lynne," my mother would say. I was the equivalent of the Saudi religious police for this courting couple.

I would stand outside the door of the lounge and burst in shouting, "Surprise, Surprise!" Can you imagine that I survived to age nine?

★★★

This was the brother who had a string of eligible friends, eminently eligible for a younger sister – she who had a crush on Dr Kildare.

These young bachelors were the highlight of the NSPCC dinner dances. They were aged twenty three or four – older men, to one who struggled to walk on her first high heels. They danced with me, those substitute Dr Kildares.

If I had a dance card it would have been filled up. It was glorious. I was in my thirties before I found out that my mother had been liberal in giving these young Fred Astaires, an appropriate and secret reward.

They had been given at the beginning of the evening, handfuls of Green Shield Stamps!

Was there something in my personality, that saw an innocence in the face of reality, or was I just plain naïve?

★★★

My summer holidays were quite unlike those of my contemporaries. I waited expectantly every year for my trip to Ile de Ré, in France; this was a magnificent small island on the west coast. It was the Charente Maritime area of France – a few miles off the coast of La Rochelle.

I had answered an advert in a school magazine for a pen friend. I received a letter back from a 'Janick Amelin' whose first letter in English began, "I am a cat." We corresponded frequently from the age of eleven (if we could call it that; how much of the other's language we actually understood, is a mystery).

Then, one day, a letter arrived from Janick, asking if she could come and stay.

My non-French-speaking mother took the train to London and met her at Paddington, where with numbered labels, families and children were matched up. She telephoned home to say all was well. Her first words were halting, the Welsh voice trembled,

"She has pierced ears!"

In those days in Neath, South Wales, that was the equivalent of tattoos, multiple piercing, and orange hair.

Fears were soon allayed.

Janick and I, hit it off immediately.

Her family was exactly like mine, only in French. Her mother shouted at her father except it was in a different language.

Ile de Ré, of my childhood, was not the new 'St Tropez' as it is today, it was *old* France. The donkeys wore long culottes; we picked grapes and trod on them.

Whatever time of day I visited the neighbours, they brought out the ubiquitous *'Pineau'*, the fortified local wine, somewhat like sherry. Each house extolling the merits, with typical French pride (or arrogance), and trying to outdo the others.

★★★

I was fourteen, life could not be better. What does one keep in the box of treasured moments?

Memories of early trips to France, the notes, the theatre tickets, the photos, the cards, the old records of singers, long dead whom no-one now recognizes.

There was France and there was life back in Wales.

My early memories there are somewhat dominated by superstition and by tea leaves. My mother's family, "the Morgans," seemed steeped in superstition. It was pervasive.

I never did, quite work it all out.

It seemed a random choice – no birds in the house. No singing before breakfast – or you will cry before the night. No shoes on the table (eminently sensible). No opening of umbrellas in the house. No major decisions on a Friday (heaven forbid) and certainly not on the thirteenth.

You would have to say "White Rabbits," White Rabbits before, or on, the first of a month. Why this applied, to even December, is beyond me!

How decisions were made seemed muddled. My mother had seen to it that we were encouraged to go to church, but I don't think the Almighty was consulted on anything in actuality.

Auntie Peggy was the oracle of choice. "Ask Peggy to come around," my father would say. My father would sit in the car reading newspapers while we were at church, so Auntie Peggy and the tarot cards did not present a conflict.

She would arrive, then came the drinking of endless cups of tea (this was in the pre tea-bag days). There would be much swirling of the dregs, and then there would be the turning upside down of the cups.

This was a serious business. Many of my family's major decisions seemed to be made in this way.

It all seemed perfectly normal at the time. Life in 'Feng Shui' style Wales.

QUESTIONS:

The author writes of her 'box' of treasured moments.

If you had such a box, what would you put in it?

What are some of the earliest memories of your childhood?

Are they of your home, friends, or perhaps of something more unfamiliar?

'Reading the tea leaves' was a ritual for this family.

What are some of your family rituals or superstitions?

Chapter Four

LEARNING DISTORTION

How did my feminine awareness begin, before eventual motherhood? My acquaintance with the facts of life had been a little skewed from the beginning. "You know right, you know wrong" was the mantra of my mother.

I will never forget that Thursday morning when I awoke to find that devastating stain on my flannelette nightdress. I was twelve, what had happened in the night?

If menstruation had been a topic at our heavily frog-oriented Biology classes, I was absent that day! I cannot remember the words of my mother when I show her the dreaded fabric stain.

An hour later, (I have by now realised that I will not bleed to death) we make a trip to the chemist. Once there, we wait ten minutes for *a girl* to serve us, and the deed is done.

I go to school with a neatly wrapped packet of what seemed like adult nappies in my school bag. What was happening to my body?

That is where Fifi comes in. She was to play an extraordinary role of tutelage.

"Thank you God for Fifi."

Fifi was our Miniature black poodle, the canine equivalent of *Gray's Anatomy for Medical Students.*

Fifi was 'in season' and later that day after school, in a mother-daughter session, I was told I was *like the dog!*

That was the entirety of my home training on the facts of life. I was in college before I seriously realized that perhaps I was not *like the dog,* I didn't have to be kept in when I had a period!

Looking back I am amazed that smart old me, was pretty stupid when it came to some things. Street smart – I was not, not even paving stone smart.

How many T.V. programmes did I miss in my youth, because my mother stood right in front of the screen when something, she judged, 'inappropriate' was being shown?

I have missed the crucial parts of more films and serials than anyone I know!

★★★

My experience of the contortions of sexual self-discovery was spending an hour standing on the seat of a Cardiff toilet trying to manoeuvre a tampon into its destination. Outside the cubicle three loyal friends shouted the biological equivalent of 'Sat. Nav.' instructions.

Years, later, thirty years later in fact, I will be eternally grateful for Princeton Seminary – Sex Week.

Glorious Sex Week! The week that filled in blanks, blanks which I didn't even know existed. There we sat seminarians and medical students in the lecture theatre at Robert Wood Johnson Teaching Hospital in New Brunswick.

We sat there listening to real, in the flesh people, willing to talk about their sexuality. There were eating-breathing transvestites, homosexuals, transsexuals, sadists, masochists, hookers and un-hookers, piercers and pimps, rubber and shoe fetish addicts, cross-dressers and self-mutilators, and every continuum in between!

Between sips of coffee, they would tell their stories and struggles. Never more, will I be embarrassed by any situation in counselling. Now I am assured and confident.

Never again would I bat an eyelid. Not in any situation, in any parish, society or any of life's revelations, or little surprises.

I had received a crash course. I had arrived. Fifi, poodle friend, I don't need you anymore!

★★★

Inter-relationships, the dynamic between a man and a woman. This brings me to that fateful meeting which was to determine the course of my life, for the next four decades, when Dorothy Judith Davies met David Michael Thomas at that B.P. Llandarcy Refinery.

That was the day my intuition was switched off, and Glorious Sex Week training hadn't yet occurred.

It was 1968, my Honours degree in English was finished, I returned to Cardiff for a year's postgraduate course in Personnel Management.

Now, I was doing a month's holiday job at a refinery nearby.

He had finished his Engineering degree at Swansea and was working the industrial part of his BP Oil Company sponsorship before continuing to do an MA at Lancaster University.

19

At the refinery, there were social events to be organized for such students. I used to say I was the social event and he was the student. He was dressed in a red sweater, he had black hair. He looked so French.

To one who was a Francophile, this alone might have skewed my judgment. He was, as we would say in Wales, a 'tidy' boy from a 'tidy' family. Like me, he had studied. I was in awe, he had graduated with a First Class Honours. He was an only child, from Carmarthen; he was respectable, eminently presentable.

Someone I could take home.

There was to continue a courtship, in the loosest sense of the word, a courtship by long distance.

He, in Lancaster, and me in Cardiff. He, in London, and me, in my first job, at Cwmbran, Mid-Wales. We wrote letters, and we talked on the phone. The word 'passion' did not even come into it.

I remember so well the nurse at the Cwmbran factory where I worked who, when I spoke of seeing him, said I should be 'fighting him off'. It never happened.

Why write about such intimacies? Over the years of hearing women's stories, I am so very aware that mine was not unique. I suppose I reflected a generational reluctance. A naïveté, which was to see thirty two years of my life take a certain direction.

What I took to be 'respect' in this courtship was nothing of the kind.

★★★

We visited France, driving down, we booked two rooms – and we stayed in two rooms.

"You know right, you know wrong" this had been hammered into me, and this was a 'tidy' boy, one who crossed, not ever a line.

All this would come flooding back when a few months into our marriage, months of marriage nothingness, *he* saw a doctor. The only advice was "Get *her* to wear a black nightie and *you* drink a bottle of wine."

It seems like yesterday. Crossing the Channel on our honeymoon, where that night we slept in separate bunks, and for two weeks I remained in pristine condition. Over the years, thirty two of them in this lonely marriage, I have wondered why smart old me never had the inkling that all was not well in the kingdom.

Then the past comes flooding back. After ten years of marriage, I still have no children.

The uncensored version of my Thomas life adds "Caused by a spouse who, on the honeymoon, and for weeks after touched you not."

I realize now, and understand now, 'non-consummation.' I have heard and understand now, the word 'annulment.' Back then, it was a private problem.

Should this be in the 'open to the world' version of my life?

Yes, yes and yes! The heartbreak it brought screams out for my present honesty. Never to be desired. No one knew, I never said.

★★★

Why did my mother, all powerful Queen Bee, this capable all intuitive matriarch not offer me saving advice.

I plaintively asked her, in a life review, some decades later.

"You would never have listened," she said.

Me, who was ninety-nine per cent on the compliant scale, *me* who wore the wedding dress and the hairstyle that I hated, but which my mother adored, *Me*?

I don't think so. I was all so obedient.

In the moments of looking back, I discover how it all unfolds, placing those vital pieces in the giant puzzle, those "aha" moments when something seems to make sense.

He had cried after that first French holiday. Sitting, head in hands at Paddington station, he had wept and said, "I don't know why I am like this. I promise I will never contact you again unless I am different."

We finished there and then, on Platform 4.

***

I went off to Cambridge, to a new job. Six months later, while I am attending a Training Course in London, he appears. Maybe it was the bunch of flowers and the box of Lindt chocolates. Maybe it was his demeanour, which seemed to indicate he had the flu, maybe it was a week of pleading.

"Make your mind up, are we getting married, yes or no?"

I gave in.

I was the only female on that two week course. There was no other woman around, off whom, I could bounce my thoughts and reservations, no one to put it into perspective.

No Auntie Peggy with the tea leaves.

I had said 'yes.'

He bought the engagement ring the next day. Then he went back to London, me to Mid-Wales. A year later we were finally in one place together – at our wedding.

The only pre-marital counselling given to us was on how we needed our Baptism certificates and proof that we had been confirmed. When I was leaving for the church that day with my father, I felt sick inside.

"Too late," said Dad.

He took my other hand in his, squeezed it and said; "If he hits you, come home."

Then off I went to be joined in holy matrimony.

QUESTIONS:

The author writes of some difficult issues.

How do you think she has coped with them?

Are there areas of her experience which resonate with yours?

How comfortable are you discussing issues of sexuality?

How important do you consider pre-marital counselling to be?

Chapter Five

HYACINTH MOMENTS

How do we move on? How does anyone deal with a chapter in their lives which affects their whole being? How does one heal life chapters and times, so devastating, that it seems the memories are carved forever?

My pain seemed so much less than the stories of those I heard. Yet it was *my* pain and it hurt. I thought of some of those early women in my life and I tried to distil their wisdom.

There have been women who have shared their stories and pain with me in a way I shall never forget. Hyacinth was one of those very special people.

There I was, a young married woman. We had returned to Swansea after the non-honeymoon. We moved into our lovely home, just off the Mumbles Road.

Michael was now working on an industrially based PhD with Aston University, his earlier degree, the Lancaster University MA, had been completed. During the day, he worked at BP Chemicals, Baglan Bay. The PhD would take all his evening hours, studying at home. It was like giving birth to an elephant. It would last almost four years. During this time, I worked as a Personnel Officer in a factory making carbon brushes for motors.

It was here that I was to meet Hyacinth.

★★★

She sat before me in my office.

'Hyacinth' was a machine operator, I had recruited her some months previously.

Her name has been indelibly etched on my brain. The chances of meeting a Jamaican woman, let alone one with such an unforgettable name in those days, were slim.

I had only seen a black person very infrequently and none before my mid-teens. I remembered Hyacinth.

"Please help me find a flat," she asked.

Racism, prejudice – the thought of trying to find Hyacinth a flat was next to Herculean in difficulty. It was later that I discovered that the flat was to be, not only for her, but for her four children.

"Why?" I queried. "Why would you want one?"

She rolled up her sleeve and there was a sight which will stay with me forever. There it was, the unmistakeable brand of an iron. I had never ever seen anything like it in my life – the wrinkled and scarred skin, a puckered, garish pink rawness against her darkness.

"He did it," she said, almost in a whisper.

She shared with me the sacred ground that was her story.

Made pregnant at sixteen by the family houseboy. Forced by her family and the shame to leave Jamaica, they had come to London, she and her illiterate husband. He had raped her many times in the marriage. She had learned to cope. After all, he was a good provider; he had never touched the children in

26

anger and had, in a weekly ritual, left his pay packet, weekly, on the mantelpiece.

Yet, his violent outbursts had become more and more frequent, the punches harder.

Then, there came the iron.

A devout Seventh Day Adventist, the only counsel given to Hyacinth by her pastor had been; "Stay. The man is the head. It is your duty."

This was my first experience of domestic violence, of abuse in all its horror. Over the years the faces in front of me have changed, so have the countries. The stories have remained the same.

★★★

In the seventies, I had heard Erin Pizzey, the feminist activist, speak in the States about violence to women. I had heard her describe in graphic detail the account of the man who had jumped on his wife as she lay on the floor and had broken most of her ribs.

Now I heard for myself the story of a different woman, Hyacinth, the woman who had been called "a fat cow" every day of her marriage, who had endured not marital bliss but marital hell.

To hear such stories, stories, 'brought to speech,' has moved me beyond measure. These were stories which transcended social groupings, ethnicity or area.

★★★

I remember the wife of a CEO of an international company. She showed me her back. He had always hit her with his fist wrapped in an iced, damp towel, so that the bruises wouldn't show.

Then there were those victims of incessant, emotional and verbal abuse, wounded by the inner scars which never showed and never healed. How do we move on?

"The body remembers," says a class colleague who, of her four sisters, was the only one raped by her father. They came back relentlessly – the flashbacks, the shivers. It is that spiral which we climb, revisiting events and yet hopefully moving upwards.

★★★

My story is not like theirs.

Three decades later, I sleep on the landing, hearing the snores which never seem to diminish and I am grateful that 'St. Michael' is, who he is. He is not in the mould of Hyacinth's violent assailant.

It is a small comfort.

Moving, moving on. Moving countries.

All the countries in which I have lived come into consciousness. In the night, in the sleeplessness, the mind goes over life chapter after life chapter.

Some seem as if they had happened only yesterday.

QUESTIONS:

What are some of the types of stories that people have shared with you?

What has been your reaction in hearing them?

What is the feeling you are left with when someone shares their pain with you?

How comfortable are you with discussing serious issues in your life?

Chapter Six

ARE YOU BEING SERVED?

Events in our lives are preparations, precursors, all part of later training.

Here I was in the early, empty days of the marriage. Michael spent the evenings in the study, working on the thesis. I suppose for him, that this was a mercy, he did not have to confront me.

Twice a week, in the evenings I taught at a local College of Further Education. I taught Psychology and managed to keep one jump ahead of the class – just. I loved it.

I had also changed my job and was now employed as a Training Officer at David Evans department store, Swansea. I moved from being a Personnel Officer in a factory, to a position as a Training Officer in a Department Store.

I had at the back of my mind that things would change when Michael had finished his studies, he would be relaxed and we would be a happy couple. I just had to hang in there in the meantime.

David Evans and the department store was an intervening chapter. Little did I realize it was the T.V. series, "Are You Being Served?" in real life!

David Evans was a family owned Department store in the centre of Swansea. It was the place you went when you wanted to buy that special wedding outfit or that very expensive gift.

It made such a difference to spend the odd moment walking around the different departments of the store rather than the noisy and often dirty environment of the factory.

It was the store which introduced me to lifts and to their hidden stories.

★★★

We had three lifts in this store of three hundred plus staff. These jobs were designated 'special' category jobs and in its benevolence, 'special' employees were placed there.

Recruitment of new lift people was therefore particularly challenging.

I employed Beryl for the Menswear lift. She was perky, chatty, a small, neat woman. She put on the uniform and had an air of professionalism. She had been with us two days. I would see her in the canteen and at tea break, all seemed well.

Some days later, a passing customer asked me,

"Is lift three working?"

"Yes," I said with conviction.

"I don't think so." retorted the customer.

I walked over to lift Number Three, Menswear. I pressed the lift button. "Coming" flashed the lift sign. The lighted sign moved up, it moved down, it moved up, it moved down, up and down, down and up, it went.

Ten minutes later the lift was still going up and down but no door was opening.

I learned right there that Beryl was a lift operator 'with attitude' as they say in the States.

Life was good for Beryl, very good, unless someone was allowed to come into her lift!

For her, satisfactory and fulfilling working conditions meant happily going up and down, down and up, until coffee and lunch breaks.

This perfect, blissful work environment would continue until the end of the day.

To Beryl, customers entering such a haven were a nuisance and to be avoided. They ruined what was her idea of the perfect job.

The next day I was looking for a replacement for lift Number Three.

★★★

Lift Number Two in Hardware had different issues. Bill had been there a year. Coming back from lunch one afternoon, I was confronted by my secretary, Paula.

"Can you please speak to this customer? There has been an incident. She is very distressed."

That year was surely the Year of the Lift Operators. Outside my office sat a weeping rotund lady, hat askew.

"Come in." I motioned and waved her politely to my office and the chair.

She was hardly through the door when it all came pouring out. Between gasps and sniffles, she eventually said, "He kissed me on the lips and told me that I was a very attractive woman."

I felt as if I had misheard, lost the plot. I eventually realized that the rotund, distressed customer in front of me was talking about herself. I needed more information.

She continued, "There were just the two of us in the lift."

It later transpired that Bill had been comforting many middle-aged, rotund customers on their attractiveness. Many a kiss had been placed on their lips with a view to cheering them up.

He saw it as something of a public service, as an act of kindness.

***

Graham was another issue.

Lift Number Two. He would stand inside his lift and at the appropriate floor and announce,

"Ground floor... Ladies shoes... handbags... *condoms*... haberdashery... and cosmetics:

Second floor: Ladies fashions... *screws*... lingerie... millinery."

It is a fact of life that when we are not expecting something, we question – did I hear what I thought I heard – we are unsure if it actually took place. It is over in a second.

How many customers had entered lift Number two, wondering their whole lives if they misheard that very peculiar floor description?

***

Lift Number One had only minor issues in comparison and they were seasonal.

Frank, the lift operator, doubled up in December as Father Christmas. We had long worked around the fact that the occasional customer or two, would mention that there was a handwritten notice up at the Santa Claus Grotto which declared, "Gone to Feed the Reindeers."

Miss Hargreaves from Haberdashery, would then have to hop it around the corner – to get Father Christmas Frank – back from the Rose and Crown!

★★★

Job descriptions are difficult to write. Unfortunately, my predecessor had not seen fit to include in the job description for Lift Number One operators, (those who double up as Father Christmas each year), that an essential ingredient in such a job description, is at least a modicum of liking and tolerance, for those smaller members of the human race!

Frank would clip them across the head in the Grotto if the list for Santa was too long. He would glower at them if the requests for toys were not what he felt was appropriate.

The small persons would be pushed off his lap at speed if they even gave a hint of wanting to touch his beard.

More interesting still, was the story recounted to me at his resignation.

On this day, when the lift had stopped at the third floor and the Grotto, Frank in his more unusually benevolent moment, had turned to his crowded group, and the small boy with them, and had announced, "Ladies and Gentlemen, and small boy, when we arrive at the next floor, I will say 'Open Sesame' you will see the doors open and a fairy will be there."

Sadly, Frank did not foresee that when the door did open, there would be, not a fairy, but a six-foot, built like-a-tank construction worker. Neither did he foresee the joyous words of the aforesaid small boy, who would exclaim, "Is this the fairy you told me about?"

I think Frank's resignation the following day had something to do with the former's comment that he was going to "bash the latter's head in."

★★★

How could the chickens I would encounter later in New Zealand ever compare with the sheer delight of characters I met at David Evans Department store? I met some unbelievable – and delightfully, eccentric characters.

David Evans Department Store had prepared me for many aspects of life. Mr Jordane, in a way that I could not have foreseen, opened my eyes and my world.

Thirty years later, in America, when I visited Dan Spence in his final moments – as he died from AIDS. I realized that many years earlier, Mr Jordane, of David Evans Department Store had long prepared the way.

★★★

Mr Jordane wasn't his real name. He was a precedent in all ways. *'Cosmetic Consultant Wanted'* read the advertisement I had placed in the local newspaper.

Forty-six applications were received. There was unbelievably one male applicant.

We are talking here about Swansea, a few miles from the valleys, from the Rugby playing mining villages. An area where men are men, where beer gets swilled by the gallon not the pint, where men break their collar bones and still stay in the scrum, where coal was delivered by the ton as if it were cotton wool in the sacks.

A male applicant! – For the cosmetic job?

He had been in administration in a factory but had thought it was a good opportunity to get into retail, which he saw as a valuable career move.

Harrods in London employed men in some of the fashion departments, I thought, "Let's go for it."

Neatly groomed, nothing untoward, the young man before me – seemed to be making indeed a good and valuable career move. The retail industry was a vast and interesting one; and here I was able to give him his chance, to move up the ladder.

He joined the following week and was given the in-store name, Mr Jordane. Orientation morning completed with other new staff, off he went and I did not give it another thought.

That was until the following week. Three giggling girls from Ladies Gloves passed me on their coffee break.

"Have you seen, Mr Jordane, today?" they grinned.

"No," I replied.

Something right there and then, told me I had better see Mr Jordane without delay. I went down to the ground floor.

For the second time in my life words did not come easily. There he was, Mr Jordane, well I think it was Mr Jordane.

This time he stood bolt upright, majestically, highlighted hair swept from his forehead, wisps of reddish hue, delicately brushed to his cheeks. The blue eye shadow and eyeliner went well with the delphinium blue silk flower on his dark blue blazer. The merest hint of eyeliner and mascara complemented the look.

Thank you God that if there was lipstick there, it was imperceptible and yet there was the faintest hint of a red Dolly Parton gloss.

"O Hello," he said. "I am just off to lunch."

He grasped a beige clutch bag on which was pinned another silk flower, he wound his lavender silk scarf around his neck, and he was gone.

He had gone only a few steps when he hesitated, turned and came back.

He whispered in my ear, "I must tell you. The counter area of that bitch in Max Factor is so dirty that you could grow mushrooms on it," and off he went again.

How I rejoice that I had met Mr Jordane. My neat, pigeon holing of God's creatures, had been blown apart.

★★★

Thirty years later, I was to live in San Francisco at its liberated height.

I didn't bat an eyelid when fur brimmed hats, high heels and five o'clock shadows got on the bus. Transvestites, transsexuals etc., Mr Jordane, had prepared me years before.

What I do regret is that I never did get to discuss, at a deeper level his struggles, what inevitably must have been his sense of isolation and hardship.

All I know is that millinery and gloves reported record sales of silk flowers and clutch handbags – and Ladies Fashions, had a major run on lavender silk scarves.

QUESTIONS:

It seems that the department store provided a light interlude for the author as she dealt with some painful issues.

What has helped you cope with a difficult life problem?

The author mentions some 'larger than-life' characters, she has met.

What has been your experience of people who might fit into this category?

Chapter Seven

BRAXTON AND FRITES

His PhD is almost finished. Michael, I am sure, will now relax. But, something else happens and our lives take a new direction.

I had been considering changing my job, it was time. I was therefore totally surprised, when he came one day with a job advert in his hands, "If I could write my own ideal job description," he said, "this is what it would be."

It was for a subsidiary of an American computer consultancy named Bonner and Moore, based in Brussels. He applied.

That first phone call and job offer from Belgium, almost thirty years ago had been the beginning of it all. It was our first international phone call.

We could not sleep for excitement.

Now all these years later, I write as one who, before I leave the house, has made at least four or five calls to the States, New Zealand, Australia and the Far East.

That call from Brussels over four decades ago seems almost farcical. It had been a major topic of conversation not only in our family, but in the neighbourhood.

Excitement indeed, in those pre-internet, pre-mobile phone, pre-anything days.

41

"Judith and Michael have had a call from Belgium."

It had been the main topic of conversation at cocktail parties for a few days. "Come and visit us when you are on vacation in France," said the company head of the computer consultancy. He added, "We will hold the job offer for you until you finish the PhD."

Could B.P. – the company who had sponsored Michael for the past five years, also offer us an international assignment?

We requested an overseas position, 'No,' there was nothing, so the decision is hastened to accept the job offer and to go on the first of our many wanderings out of this green and pleasant land.

Goodbye Wales. Hello Mannikin Pis – and Frites.

★★★

Both the office and our apartment were located on Avenue Louise, designer office chic.

It was to be the beginning of my many coffees taken around The Grand Place. The whole area was all permutations of items made in Brussels lace. You name it, there it was made in the finest 'dentelle.' It was the city of bus tours, tourists who would descend and gather around that small statue of a small boy peeing, the famous 'Mannikin Pis'.

What perverse sculptor would plan to make a statue of a small boy answering the call of nature? Yet there it is a national symbol.

My life was to be vibrant. Michael travelled two weeks out of every month to a refinery in 'Kraluupy' near Prague.

His previous BP experience held him in good stead.

He was one of a small group of technical experts in his field. His travelling meant that two weekends every month were gone from our lives.

I sought something to occupy me.

★★★

How fortuitous therefore that one 'Braxton Foxe, Personnel Director' lived in the same building, his company offices on the top floor.

Braxton was the Personnel Director for a large combine harvesting company in Kansas. He had been assigned to establish the company's European offices in Brussels.

He needed a French speaking P.A.

He got a Welsh one – me.

It was Braxton's first oversees assignment. Life was very different away from Kansas, and the small company town making the farm equipment.

One got the impression that for Braxton to go to Europe was titillating, he had taken a wicked decision to work in an unknown and decadent world far from the safety and cleanliness of good – of that good old Kansas town.

He had brought with him, Mary Beth, his wife and three young sons, Rick, Robby and Ron (I mused how the family sorted their overseas mail which arrived 'Master R. Foxe').

Braxton was the first 'real' 'American, as they say, to whom I had spoken more than just a passing "Hello." I surely was, for him, the first living and breathing specimen of the Warrior Race.

Fluent in French, from my many childhood times on Ile de Ré, I assisted Braxton. I did not type; he had a secretary, Francoise for that.

I was on special assignments.

For Braxton, Brussels was surely another planet. I am not sure how much work he actually did. Every receipt, every small expense, even the few centimes needed for a public toilet was lovingly noted by him in a notebook he carried with him.

"It was hard living in this Godforsaken Belgium, and if Mary Beth needed to spend an hour on the phone to Kansas to arrange her beauty shop appointment in a month's time, so be it."

These were legitimate and justifiable expenses.

Mary Beth had been for me, an apocryphal figure until the time when we actually met.

"Judith," said a wistful Braxton, "You know where the neighbourhood launderette is. Go down to our apartment on the third floor and tell Mary Beth how to get there."

As I said, the office was in the same building on the eighth floor. It was one of life's conundrums that it must have been very hard for Braxton to consistently arrive late each morning, on the journey from the third to the eighth floor.

Off I trundled, down to the third floor, pressing the bell and waiting excitedly at the thought of at last seeing the marital partner of the Foxe household.

I knock at the door.

I am not sure if Kansas is classed as a Southern state but it was a Southern Belle who answered. The other half of the Foxe partnership opens, full makeup from mascara to powdered cheeks, coiffed and sprayed stiff, a dress that Dorothy on the yellow brick road would have been proud of.

"Mary Beth," says me, the 'Celtic Sat. Nav.'

"Braxton asked me to pass on to you the directions for the launderette."

I then proceeded for the next few minutes, with my Welsh lilt, to give explicit directions to the facility.

She looked blankly at me. Eyeball to eyeball. Then in a slow, paced, every syllable pronounced sentence said,

"I don't speak French."

★★★

There have been less than a handful of times in my life when I have been lost for words, and this was one of them. Here I was, living specimen of the Welsh Warrior Race with accent to match, speaking the Queen's English!

Would she have said the same to a Richard Burton or a passing Tom Jones?

Belgium was the beginning of a life enriched by understanding cultural divides. The Foxes also taught me another thing. Braxton taught me work 'savvy,' he taught me the intricacies of the world of Personnel and Human Relations in a way that I had never fathomed.

Certainly not anything that was taught in my Cardiff postgraduate course of Personnel Management.

I would go into Braxton's office and he would be intently looking at a letter.

"Judith," he would say pensively, "I have had an application letter from some man in Germany, in Bavaria.

I don't think it is fair to ask him to come all the way to Brussels for an interview. Can you check out how I can get there, stay a few days?

I wonder if Mary Beth could spare the time to help me out on it. I'll ring her, maybe she could visit with me."

Braxton, wanted to spare all these tired and stressed applicants the long haul trip to Brussels, in Belgium. Brussels in fact, was to visit the letter writers in Rome, Geneva, Nice and Salzburg, etc.

I was glad that Mary Beth, providentially, was able to fit it in her timetable to accompany him, and fortuitously those seeking employment with Haughton International – would write their letters at times – that would fortuitously coincide with Rick, Robbie and Ron's school breaks.

Brussels was my glass ceiling experience.

★★★

Later I joined Gascoigne S.P.R.L. I was a training consultant. I visited many company headquarters in Brussels doing studies in and outside company training.

I remember visiting Liggett and Myers.

The person in front of me was a young man of about thirty, American.

"I suppose," he said, (in that – 'I have just completed three takeover bids this morning,' voice), "that in your training you are using CCTV," – which was real up to date technology then.

"No," I said, dismissively, with only half a withering look learned from 'Queen Bee' my Welsh 'dominating mother', "I use the new method."

I did not go into details to explain that the 'new method' was *me*! As a little Chickadee sitting in front of him, I reflected that the Harvard MBA course he attended, probably had a section headed, "Note for all New Executives: Never Show Ignorance."

Checkmate. Harvard!

I and the so – called 'New Method' win!

QUESTIONS:

When in your life have you experienced a different culture?

The author writes of her life as vibrant.

What, if any have been the times when you would use this word to describe your life?

What have been some of the amusing stories in your work experience?

Chapter Eight

DEVASTATION IN A WHITE MACK

Carole was a British friend I met in my early days in Brussels. I was still working at Gascoigne as a Training Consultant.

She had lived in Belgium for some time. We would meet for lunches and for coffee. Her husband worked in Saudi Arabia on contract, and when her two children were in school, we would meet – scheduling permitting – for adorably long coffee chats around the Grand Place.

It felt reminiscent of the Grand Époque, give or take the inevitable American tourists milling around. We enjoyed our chats and discussions, me talking about my various work incidences, she on the various aspects of life in the bustling capital.

In looking back over my life chapters, I see that there have been times when I have hidden so well the pains of my heart.

There in a marriage which I describe as "talking to myself." I did not identify those similar lonely spots in others, nor did I confide to others my own.

I did not see that Carol and Michael might in a bizarre week, which was to occur, might discover the means of confronting their own issues.

It did not occur to me that in asking him to take her home one evening after a meal with us, that it would open some unforeseen floodgate.

Their affair lasted five days.

★★★

I came back from a visit to England, to be met at the Central Bus Station by Carole, who told me starkly that she and Michael had spent most of those days which I was away, as "man and wife."

Each evening she had arranged babysitting with her neighbour and had gone to our apartment. She also said something which I have quietly smiled over during the years. She said, "It was all like an interview."

In some way this confirmed something deep in my feelings. This was truly devastation in a 'white mackintosh' (she often wore one). At the time, I suppose it would fall into a category of a matrimonial post-traumatic shock. Shocked out of my socks, I was!

Amazingly, I did not hate her, I did not feel badly towards her, it affirmed, confirmed, something that I could not quite put my finger on.

I spent that night checked into a hotel, asking my Belgian friend, Viviane, to go to my apartment and to deliver my clothes and documents to me so that I could leave Belgium.

I now longed to just leave it for ever.

Michael, however, was there in the apartment when she arrived with my key. The documents and clothes stayed in the drawer.

He would not give them to her. I duly returned.

I remember that for the next months, I seemed to spend my lunches and dinners alternating between eating McVities Digestives and huge plates of Spaghetti Bolognese.

I alternated between private weeping, drinking red wine with my colleague, Sheila, and intense anger that he did not want *me,* but could want someone else.

When Carole's husband returned from Saudi, Michael went to see him, he confessed this "dreadful mistake" and we did not see either of them ever again.

It ended as we would say in Wales, 'tidily.'

***

This was not the proverbial seven year itch; this was the shocking, devastating four year itch. It was to take years to get over, the anger, the hurt, the betrayal.

Surprisingly, I found that over and over, the anger was not directed towards Carole, but towards the situation in which I found myself, trapped as before, where nothing changed.

My sense of self had been 'bashed' that was for sure.

He hadn't felt passion for me, and yet it seemed neither did he for her. "It was all like an interview" was hardly 'coup de foudre' material, not the style of grand romance.

It had been betrayal of the deepest kind, by a husband and by a friend.

I did not see any emotional regret in him, just indifference, and nothingness.

It was done and dusted and we carried on.

I did not tell our families, after all we were far away in Belgium. To the day they died, Michael was still 'St Michael' to his parents and his Auntie Gwladys. It was not until much later, that the shame of divorce was to confront them. He remained, as always in their eyes, totally virtuous, evident sainthood.

He and I continued as before, apart from my moments of uncontrollable weeping. I inwardly processed it all, I missed my coffees and lunches with (what must have been without my realizing it), a lonely and unhappy Carole.

He would still spend two weeks out of every month in Czechoslovakia, and I continued my training work at Place Madou.

Over the years, I have counselled many couples and individuals in their marriages. Can affairs in marriages be surmounted?

I know they can.

What I now realize is that mine was not a close couple marriage, rocked by the shock and pain of an outside relationship.

Mine was a distant soliloquy where 'one flesh' had never been an actuality. My little life, however, had been shaken to its core by these events beyond my control. What was I going to do for the rest of it?

QUESTIONS:

What do you imagine would have been your reaction to the events described?

Do you think she was right to stay?

How would you have dealt with betrayal by a friend?

How do you deal in your life with the concept and the practicality of forgiveness?

What have been the times in your life, when you have had to do this?

Chapter Nine

PRINCETON AND PIETY

Our time in Brussels was ended, my long coffee meetings at The Grand Place had long since lost any joy for me.

The company of Bonner and More was relocating back to Texas. We had misgivings but an available job opportunity with Mobil Oil meant that Michael would be offered a position with them, and we would go to America for one year's orientation before a posting back to the U.K.

It was the best of both worlds. We were to be orientated, Americanized, in Princeton. Wonderful, Ivy League University, old money town, Princeton in New Jersey.

Princeton was everything that I loved. I was not able to work due to the restrictive nature of Michael's visa. I was a lady of leisure. As we rented in the town itself, I took full advantage of the concession to attend university lectures free of charge. I joined the 'Newcomers' Group.

We had met a couple, we rented their old apartment and this time, in her, I found someone with whom I could share. She also was in a marriage, without the infidelity, but with the same underlying loneliness, the same sense of rejection as mine.

We met and we talked, we talked and we met.

It was cathartic.

My friendship experience with Carole was never to prevent me making close women friends in the future, if anything it made the friendships and the sharing time more meaningful.

I was more aware of the wounds we all carry.

★★★

It was in Princeton, however, that another event shook my very foundations. Big 'G' came onto the scene, centre stage and big, big time. Life was never to be the same ever again. God, Father, Son and Holy Ghost, prayer book designation, burst into my existence.

We were renting an apartment in the centre of town, while signing for our apartment lease; we went to the Lamplighter bookstore, owned by our landlord.

As I looked around I could see that it was one of '*those*' shops – a religious bookstore. Cringe.

"If you want to borrow any books, feel free."

I was a voracious reader, but these titles were something else.

In good old England, we kept our faith to ourselves. Christened in cold and draughty parish churches at ages we could never remember, we were very quiet about any supernatural activity.

This was the good old Church of England, appearing if at all, in one's life. My father, after all, had preferred to sit in the car during service time following the religion of the Sunday Express and the News of the World.

The book titles I saw around me now were out of my experience – "God's Warrior," "Life in the Spirit," "Spiritual Warfare."

We certainly didn't talk about such things back home in Wales. That was for the fiery cross 'loonies.'

Yet, I borrowed books. I borrowed the books about the Old Testament, about the New Testament, I borrowed books about martyrs, about missionaries, about saints, about sinners, and I borrowed books about death, judgement, Heaven, Hell and umpteen aspects in between.

I read about the person of Christ, what he did, what he said, to whom he said it and why.

I had a desire to read, more an insatiable desire to read these spiritual tomes.

From basic to complicated.

I suppose I may have wanted to make sense of what had happened to me in Belgium.

I went further than reading these inspirational and devotional books, I started to read the *text* itself. Something changed inside.

Six weeks later, I was absolutely convinced that I should study Theology and at some convenient point enter some form of full time ministry!

★★★

My life changed at that point. There was no flash of lightning from above, no audible voices, but Big 'G', Son and the Holy Ghost, became more real than those around me.

The proof, as they say is in the pudding.

It was not for three and a half decades later that I would finally be 'Reverend Dr' and would put as my occupation, 'Clergy.'

Ending up with three theological degrees on my office wall; two Masters from Princeton, and a Doctorate from San Francisco.

Why did this all happen in Princeton?

The 'White Mack Moment' had shaken my whole world.

Nothing had happened as I had expected or planned. I had been bowled over because never in a million years had I expected anything like that. I had been a good girl, Carole was a good girl. Even 'St Michael' had been a chapel goer!

I may have tried to equate all this with that concept of sinful acts, who knows. In my reading, I looked deeper into the human condition, what makes us tick, our motives, joys and sorrows.

It all went into the wash and out came an absolute conviction that there was indeed another dimension in life, a spiritual one, and I wanted to be on it, in it, with it.

I have never looked back.

★★★

I suppose it was the prayer of Humble Access writ large. "We do not presume" and I certainly was unworthy to eat any crumbs. But I had discovered the God, 'whose property is always to have mercy' I felt that I had found Him, but in actuality, He had found me.

I began a series of Theology courses by correspondence. I wrote a letter to a Reverend John Stott of All Souls, Langham

Place, London. I had read his book on Christianity which I found very impacting.

I had no idea that he was an internationally famous religious writer.

I received in return a handwritten letter from him, asking that when I returned to Britain, I might like to arrange a meeting with him.

Ten months later, I did.

He gave me as much time as I needed to talk. I talked of my readings, of this inner prompting, of this spiritual change. I told him of my feelings, of my desire for ministry (somewhat out of sync, as at this time, we did not even ordain women in England). In hindsight, his words were so wise.

"If you feel this way, do not worry that it will go away, perhaps at this moment in time God means you to stay in industry."

I took this great man's advice. I applied for some management and training jobs, and applied for a job as a Training Manager with a travel company, Wakefield Fortune, based in Southampton Row, London.

I was offered the position and accepted.

In addition, twice a week I attended an evening Theology course at Southwark. This was a two-pronged approach. God has a sense of humour. That I know for sure.

My position at Wakefield Fortune was to turn out quite differently from what I had expected and certainly from what I had imagined.

★★★

It was about seven one evening. I worked late; I was the only one, or so I thought, in the office. I could hear noise from along the corridor. I had no idea what to expect. The door of John's office (my boss) was slightly open and there he sat at his desk, head in hands.

I realized that the sounds I had heard were his sobbing.

He looked up in embarrassment.

"Well, Judith, you'd better know. Thirty years with the company, and they told me today, that's it. You're fired."

One of the things my pre-marriage, postgraduate course in Personnel Management at Cardiff University gave me was knowledge of the intricacies of Industrial Relations Law.

John and I sat and talked. We talked a long time. He listened intently. "John, you can take them to Industrial Tribunal. Here are the steps to take." I began to write some notes.

That weekend, I had decided that I had absolutely no wish to work for a company that had acted in such a despicable manner. After all, I was happy studying Theology, I was operating on a different plane!

We had no family to support, we had plenty of savings; I would give in my notice. This was a moment when Michael was totally alongside any decision I might make, and wonderfully supportive. He gave some spot-on advice.

"Fine," he said. "Whatever you decide to do is O.K. by me, but go and see the Managing Director and tell him face to face why you are making that choice."

Monday, I made the appointment to see the MD, his was the office upstairs. There are moments when I live up to my mother's designation as 'The Warrior Race.' This was one of them.

★★★

I told Mr Eric B, how appalled I was at the way my boss had been treated. Who would want to work for a company who did such things?

Secondly, importantly, in business savvy terms, it was (says me) a stupid thing to do. The Company had not followed Employment Legislation procedure, they had completely ignored all the mandatory steps required in a dismissal, serve them right – they would now end up losing at a Tribunal, and would have to pay a huge amount in compensation.

With satisfaction, I enumerated all the steps they had not taken, I went through each and every missing procedural move. He sat there quietly, then, looked at me with an expression that I could not quite define and said, "Thank you, Mrs Thomas. You seem very knowledgeable about these things, Goodbye." (I think the latter part was said 'tongue in cheek.') and he quickly opened the door to usher me out into the corridor, quickly returning to pick up his phone and make a call.

Off I went again – the arrogance of youth, talking at length on Employment Law and Procedure. I, who was into Deuteronomy and Daniel, Gospels and God, I was on the Theology Fast Track future.

God of the Gospels, however, as I said, has a sense of humour. Three weeks later John the Boss, was given a very substantial, out of court settlement, and I got promoted to Personnel and Training Director with a company car.

I deemed this a divine sign, that Big G certainly wanted me to stay in industry!

Following these events, I was consulted by the company on all matters of dismissals and downsizing. I, who was 'geographically challenged,' had to practice with weekend trips, in my bright, grey, shiny company car. Every weekend I practiced how to drive to the travel agents that I would have to visit during the week!

Mr Eric B, MD, said I was the only one in his whole career who had begged him, *not* to have a company car, "Could I go by train, instead?" I had asked.

I certainly was, he said, 'Different.'

Once a month, I would fly up to Glasgow to visit the part of the company there. I instituted comprehensive new Management courses for the fifty seven travel shops in the company, I drew up counter training evaluations. We put in new feedback procedures, training courses to the right – and training courses to the left.

All this in tandem with New Testament Theology and Greek studies, twice weekly, in Southwark Diocese. Holy Spirit at work literally!

QUESTIONS:

Has faith been part of your journey?

The author writes that the circumstances in which she found herself were a fertile time for spiritual reflection.

What have been some of the situations in your life where you may have said the same?

How difficult do you consider it is to live out one's faith in a normal work situation?

Chapter Ten

JAPAN AND LOTUS BLOSSOM

The days in my company car passed merrily. Other days I commuted to Southampton Row, and duly nodded off with all the other commuters in the carriage on the way back. Michael spent his time between the office in Victoria and the refinery at Coryton.

Life as we all know is not straightforward. It was John Lennon who said, "Life is what happens to you when you are busy making other plans." We were to experience one of those 'off piste' life moments.

It was a Friday evening. Dan Dowling, Michael's boss was being transferred to Japan in a few weeks and we were out celebrating with him and his wife. They were delighted and happy for this new move in his career. He was in his mid-forties and it seemed wonderful news, their two teenage children were over the moon with excitement.

On the Monday morning, I received a call at the office from Michael. He spoke slowly, "Dan Dowling has dropped dead." Nowadays, we hear of sudden, inexplicable 'heart deaths.' Then they did not hit the headlines. It was unbelievable.

Life has ways of shaking us around and around.

***

Dan's death was to result in Michael and myself being asked to go to Japan in his place. We were easy to move, no children in school, we were willing, eager and mentally packed.

We had been in London almost three years by this time; the opportunity to visit far flung Japan was to be seized. Marriage decisions on hold – we are off to travel!

Japan was one of those countries that I had longed to visit since forever. Geisha, Samurai, Tea-ceremony, Kimonos, whatever it had to offer, I wanted to see and experience it all.

We had a large, spacious, downtown apartment in the chic *Omotesando* area. This was the equivalent to living on the Champs Elysées in Paris. Michael went every day to the refinery in Yokohama, I threw myself into language classes, all day and every day (at the same time, still completing and sending correspondence Theology courses back to England).

When an American acquaintance told me that she was returning for two years to America with her husband, she advised me to apply for her job at Mitaka Women's University outside Tokyo. I did and got the position.

***

Two days a week teaching English in its broadest sense, language, culture and literature. There I met, what was to me, the enigma that were Japanese women university students.

I had to take three trains to get to *'Mussashi no Joshi Daigaku'*, a private Buddhist Women's University at Mitaka.

I had once read a book called "One Step Behind" about the role of women.

Many of the Japanese language words embraced intrinsically the idea that women were not perhaps anywhere equal to men. A daughter-in-law would be the last to use the family hot bath, the *ofuro*.

I recall my American friend, married to a Japanese man who called the police when he hadn't returned home that evening, nor had she heard a word from him the next day.

She was frantic, and staggered when she was told that a typical Japanese wife waited three days before making such a call!

Japan in the late seventies!

I was enjoying life. I was the University's first native English teacher. Who knows how many Japanese families have mothers who now enunciate with a Welsh accent!

I had been thrown off balance, when after professionally outlining the syllabus for that year, the two questions they asked were, "How old are you?" and "Is your husband handsome?"

The young women were dressed in pop socks, Mickey Mouse sweaters, they adored Western things. Many of them told me they were having arranged marriages. Few had long term career objectives.

Such was the time and culture.

★★★

I also helped my American friend with overspill of her language students. Some were telephone lessons, for others I would visit their homes.

★★★

By this time, I had been visiting Professor Hiroshi Iwanaga for two years. I had inherited him from my friend Jan, who had never actually met him in person. She had only spoken to him on two occasions.

He wanted to talk about his subject – Middle Eastern History, Religion and Culture – with a native speaker. He got one, *me*.

Professor Iwanaga must have been in his late sixties when I first met him. It was very hard to accurately guess his age. During my time of visiting over the months, his hair went dramatically from a light grey to deep black in a day!

He had however not, as many men did in Tokyo at that time, 'permed' it. Naively, I had daily wondered why so many of the so called '*salarymen*' that I passed each day sported curls.

A Japanese friend confided, "Perms."

Iwanaga San was fluent in Arabic, had written many books on his subject. His college teacher had been a Cambridge don.

I spent hours in preparation pouring through Newsweek, Encyclopaedias and other sources to prepare and start our lessons. If I asked one good question, he would be off like the 'Duracell Battery Rabbit,' he would talk for hours.

"Professor," I would begin, "Please tell me how the Abbasid dynasty developed in the twelfth century."

I would then mention the most obscure minutiae relating to a little known aspect – and we were off!

I was spellbound.

He would begin faultlessly. He would deliver for the two hours of the lesson a lecture in beautiful English. If I asked at the end of it, if he had had a good weekend, he would be speechless.

He was unable, to formulate, even the most basic social sentence of reply.

Chit chat was not part of Iwanaga San's curriculum.

Mitaka days, Iwanaga days, Japanese lesson days, Sushi and Sashimi days, writing down how many women I saw in kimono days... I loved them all.

★★★

The marriage issue was on one track that seemed destined to go nowhere. It was, however, all negative, the offending reasons buried, ten years, into the marriage monologue.

My desire, however, to have children was different. That was growing.

It seems inconceivable now that we did not discuss with any professional who tried to help us with our infertility issue, that maybe a predominant reason for our non-producing was that we hardly ever had intercourse!

It was something that was just not mentioned.

Mercifully, times have changed! Seeing the wonderful *kodomos*, (children) around us, and the *akachans* (babies), maybe here, in Japan, something would be different.

I raised the issue of adoption. Michael agreed unreservedly.

We put our names down with a large government adoption agency. During the months, we were screened financially, socially, and every which way.

Ten years and no children were proof enough for the Japanese. If there should be a possibility that a child might be available, what would we consider, racially, age wise?

We would respond, "Aged zero to two, boy or girl. Nationality mix unimportant."

Two years passed, since the day, we had first put our names down with the agency. It had been months of interviews, papers submitted, all requirements had now long ago been completed.

We had waited... and waited... and waited.

Our time in Japan was now over. A month to go, we had given notice on our apartment, Michael's task force work was over, and I had two weeks left at the University.

We were ready to move on.

★★★

In the spiritual part of my life, Japan had been invigorating. I had attended lectures at Sophia University on Zen and Catholicism, I had enjoyed Bible studies with ladies from all denominations and nationalities.

Since my time in Princeton, prayer was now an integral part of my life. I was a lay reader at St Albans' Anglican church. Tuesdays, I had a daytime Bible study at our apartment. I had friends with whom I shared most of the deepest longings of my heart.

One afternoon I had prayed with two of them about the unfulfilled desire for children. I knew the biblical prayer of Hannah for a child, off by heart.

Prayer partners – fervent Pam Pak and equally fervent

Geri Miller – sat holding hands, white knuckled, grasping my Welsh hand in theirs.

"Ten years and nothing, no babies," declares solemnly wonderfully evangelical Pam Pak, an American woman married to a Korean.

"God will deal with this," she announced with authority as if she had just received a directive from the Almighty Himself.

"Let us pray about *your* birth."

Why pray about *my* birth, I was the one trying to get pregnant!

Was God, I wondered up for all this? It would be some months later that this aspect of my birth would click into context. I will explain later.

It would be in an American walk-in wardrobe, years, and years later that it would all make sense to me – why this particular prayer would be vitally significant.

Then it just seemed odd.

Yet, miraculously, there and then, in that Tokyo apartment, in a way I will never, ever, understand, it was as if a gear moved in heaven.

It seemed as if a re–filing in the heavenly 'Family Application Drawer' had just happened and my request got pushed immediately to the front and marked, "urgent."

Was this an example of divine synergy in action?

★★★

About that time in Tokyo, two Japanese students – a twenty year old boy and an eighteen year old girl go to a hotel in Shinjuku – and Japanese citizen, girl baby is conceived.

Later to be known as – 'Alison Rachel Thomas' she is ready to enter my 'Corporate Exxon Mobil' world, child Number One.

My first, wonderful blessing of motherhood would happen without the customary nine months preparation. I was about to be an instant mother. There were no piles of baby books next to the bed – on 'when to burp, or when to change, or to feed.'

Nine months later, Michael and I were to be proud parents of an eight day old Japanese baby girl, born December 4th 1980. She arrived permanently to reside with us a week later.

How did it all unfold?

It was two weeks before the end of term; I had just got back to the apartment to find that there was a message for me at the front desk. "Thomas San. Your husband has been trying to contact you. Please go to this address by 4.30 today. Urgent."

It was the address of the adoption agency.

I hurriedly put my coat back on, and made my way to the subway station again. Michael and I arrived at the adoption office almost simultaneously, with no time to talk to each other.

Miss Kondo a strikingly tall, Japanese woman with a very pleasant and approachable manner was there waiting. She had finished her Master's degree in America, her English was fluent. She had been our contact throughout the whole process, she knew us, we liked and trusted her. She said slowly, "Please sit down, Mr and Mrs Thomas. We have just been told that we have an eight-day old, healthy Japanese baby girl available for adoption. The mother has insisted on adoption by a foreign couple."

She paused, and looked directly at Michael, then at me.

Michael said, "What's the next step?" He said it startlingly quickly, which was unusual. Even more startling was her reply.

"Decide now if you want to go ahead. If it is yes, I will go with you to the hospital tomorrow, to collect her."

"You must choose a name for her by then, as we must register her immediately. Then we will have six months to finalize everything. There will be a lot of paperwork."

We cannot relive that moment of shock. I still have in a treasured baby book the scratched note and details which Michael made in those following minutes.

A young unmarried student, refusing an early abortion, had taken the unusual step of adoption outside the family, and had contacted this agency during the pregnancy.

Here we were, numbed, being asked the million dollar question. "Yes or No?" We did not have to think, we looked at each other and we both said an emphatic, "Yes, Yes."

★★★

I cannot recall how we managed it, but we got ourselves out of the Agency office to a friend's house which was nearby. Alison and her husband were in Tokyo with Lloyds Bank International. I enjoyed afternoons with their small son, Edward, we saw them often.

I had not confided in Alison or anyone about our adoption plans. Logically, it would have made any disappointment easier to bear. Now that we had finished our assignment and we were two weeks from leaving, it wasn't an issue.

Now Alison received the news, in all its fullness. Alison was as shocked as we were. A baby tomorrow! When her husband arrived half an hour later, we were all in need of a stiff drink.

The news gradually sank in to the four of us. We had to get busy and prepare! The shops were closed by this time, no chance to buy baby clothes or indeed anything.

It is providential that heaven had *some* issues firmly in hand. We left Alison's apartment with a basic, 'pick a baby up tomorrow kit.' It didn't seem to matter that everything was blue, formerly owned by young Edward.

How we got on the right *Chikatetsu* subway train home after that I will never know.

Alone for the first time in our apartment, we sat down, dazed.

Michael was worried that he did not know enough Japanese to speak to the baby, "She's eight-days old," I reminded him, and then I promptly went on to consider appropriate names – all of them boys!

We were confused, 'in shock.' An eight-day old baby! We had never really dealt with any small creature under six months old. An hour's daze later, he said, "I like Alison."

"Yes," I said, "she's been a wonderful, invaluable help."

"No," he said, "I mean call the baby Alison."

So 'Alison Rachel' it was.

★★★

I don't think we slept at all that night, we had *lots* to do.

We went through all that was urgent – we had given notice on our apartment – Michael's project had been completed, his assignment in Tokyo was over – I had two weeks left of term – and now we were to have an instant family in a few hours!

Miss Kondo had stressed that we would be unable to leave Japan for six months until the adoption was finalized by a court order. Technically, the baby would still be under the jurisdiction of the Agency.

We would have to begin the long process with the British Embassy and Japanese officialdom. We were a precedent. No British couple had adopted a Japanese baby, a Japanese citizen. All this was going around and around in our heads, swirling with the name 'Alison Rachel.'

In ministry over the years, in hearing the stories of many women, I have reassessed what it means to be loved and to be touched.

That wonderful, indescribable gift of being able to have experienced what it means to be a mother, for us to experience parenthood. In this news, in this tremendous blessing, in this against all odds situation, how could I not give thanks to what I knew to be divine intervention?

Here I was in Japan, experiencing motherhood, Michael fatherhood, another project together other than moving. This we could manage.

The next day we had decided that he had urgently to go to the Mobil office and explain the situation.

I would go with Miss Kondo to the hospital to get the baby. If Mobil would not allow him to stay for the required six months, we or I would be facing a major issue.

I don't know quite if it had really dawned on me that I would be coming home with a small, week old, baby in my arms, but I set off for the hospital rendezvous in high heels.

Miss Kondo and I travelled the three hours or so together. It was an added joy that there, I was able to meet the doctor who had delivered this unexpected life-changing small being.

The birth mother had made the decision not to see the child, who had been taken away immediately after delivery. She had, however, left a small bag of nappies and a hand knitted, yellow jacket.

I could not help but shed tears when I saw the little warm coat, made I presume, by her. She had carried this child to term, given her life. That precious, precious gift she was now giving to us. I was never to meet this mother but I think about her often. I hope that she went on to marry, to have her own family. Out of her 'mistake' came one of the greatest blessings of our lives.

There was no time, however, to dwell then on such matters. After some papers were completed, a nurse entered with a blanket in which, was the person herself, a small baby with sticking up hair – absolutely gorgeous.

I can never relive that moment. It was love at first sight.

Miss Kondo, me in tottering heels, and baby, made our way back to Tokyo. I had not yet thought of this small soul as 'Alison' nor indeed did I fully grasp that in six months, God willing, she would be absolutely, totally our child.

What would Michael feel? He, of course, would be still at the office, pleading the case to stay another six months.

I knew that he would be as much in love with her as I was – and he was, and is.

★★★

As we drew near to *Omotesando* and the apartment, I had forgotten that in the rush that morning, I had telephoned down stairs, to my neighbour Ursula. I had told her where I was going and why.

Ursula had three adult sons. She and her husband, Toby, were South Africans, in Tokyo on assignment with General Motors.

By the time Miss Kondo came through the door, I looked to see my spare room decorated like a nursery.

Ursula, wonderful Ursula, had arranged to have the key and there was a cot, clothes, nappies, baby bath – everything. Some of the neighbours had small children; it was a wonderful joint apartment block effort.

Minutes later, Michael arrived. All was fixed. Mobil was one hundred per cent supportive; he could stay, albeit doing some very menial administrative jobs. Our apartment had not yet been leased, so we could also stay where we were.

Everything clicked into place.

All this was said before he looked inside the blanket in the new cot in the corner. There was the reason – very small and wrinkly, with thick, black, sticking up hair!

In the midst of all this exchange of information and nursery discovery, stunned and inquisitive neighbours were popping in an out. Then something completely bizarre, (at least it seemed to me) occurred. The baby, still in the blanket, but in the process of being passed from parent to neighbour, to neighbour to parent, this wrinkly small person started to cry.

The little soul with sticking up hair needed to be fed!

Miss Kondo was still in the apartment, discussing some

details with Michael. She reminded me that we had a can of formula recommended by the doctor and we had the bottle.

There is something to be said for motherly and grandmotherly experience.

All those neighbours knew far more than Dr Spock and his books ever would. I had, as it were, an abundance of residential District nurses, who would pop up to our apartment at any hour of the day and night and set us straight.

Ursula would come up and show me how to bathe Alison, all aspects of motherhood, how to feed, how to bathe, how to burp, how to change nappies – I was taught everything in a crash course by Ursula and Co.

The following evening, two of the Mobil project team had been invited for a meal. We had tried and tried to contact them, to cancel. They were out of town for a meeting and we were unable to reach them, knowing nothing of the event whatsoever, they arrived on schedule for what was anticipated to be a quiet supper.

I opened the apartment door; they were noisy, thrusting their bottle of wine into my hand… "Shhhhh. Be quiet, we have a baby."

When they had last seen us, a week and a half earlier, we didn't have one. Now we did.

This Japan was certainly a different kind of assignment!

★★★

Our Alison Rachel was a shock, not only to us, but to friends and neighbours, work colleagues. One of the major 'tremors' was my phone call, a day later to the University.

"I am sorry, Higuchi San, I cannot come to give lessons this week, I have a baby."

That took much, much explaining.

The next afternoon, after classes, five of the women staff came to see me, arms bursting with '*presentos.*' I still have the photograph.

I had been told by Miss Kondo, that at that time in Japanese hospitals, the name of the hospital, mother and baby would be written on the baby's foot in indelible ink. It would gradually wear off. "Do not show the underside of her foot," she said, as they will be able to read the 'kanji' and her details."

That, was of course, the very part of Alison's anatomy that the '*Mussahsi No Joshi Daigaku*' teachers wanted to see. It was almost sumo wrestling to make sure that there was no way they were going to take her bootee off and *read* the personal details of her adoption.

There was tussling, wrapping, swaddling, but no bootees came off! I won.

★★★

The reactions of the Japanese colleagues in Michael's office were equally incredulous. They could not understand the concept at all. Any illegitimate children were kept within the family; adoption was never outside the all-important blood of the family register.

At that time also, abortion was a well-used means of birth control. Some Japanese women had confided they had had six or seven.

To see this foreign couple with what looked like a Japanese baby was confusing, moreover it was impossible.

The local shopkeepers where I bought my fruit and vegetables each evening, looked at me, looked at him, looked at me, looked at the baby and then gestured that they had no idea at all that I had been pregnant!

It helped that Michael had black hair.

The courageous decision of Alison's birth mother meant that the baby would leave Japan, a new life. Alison was born on December 4th 1980, Christmas that year was exquisitely special. Michael was a doting and hands-on father. Life was good.

★★★

We took it in turns to spend hours at the British Embassy with the horrendous paperwork. Alison would not automatically be a British Citizen, we had to apply. The Japanese Family Court wanted a guarantee that she would be granted British citizenship before they would finalize the adoption.

We went around and around in circles. Mr Warren–Knott the British Consul spent hours and hours with us, and the rest of his time with a British citizen, who was in custody on a drugs charge.

He would arrive at our meetings exhausted.

"Do we know this person on the drugs charge?" we asked. The expat community of Britons at that time was not large.

"Yes, you know him."

It was Paul McCartney with marijuana.

Years later at Alison's wedding, her proud father spoke of how she had as a baby, competed for the attention of the British Consul, divided as it was, between herself and the famous Beatle.

Yet, amid the paperwork, the meetings, the getting to know this beautiful baby who slept all night at three weeks old, there was to be another absolutely mind-blowing happening in *my* life.

Really – mind blowing!

QUESTIONS:

To want a child and to experience infertility can be painful.

What advice would you give to someone in this situation?

The author writes of the unpreparedness of being an instant parent.

How do you think it must have felt to experience parenthood in this way?

What do you feel about interracial adoption? What issues, if any, would make you hesitate?

Chapter Eleven

THE UNTIDINESS OF THE
FAMILY TREE

Life chapter's neat, and life chapters untidy. What and where is
a beginning? Where and what is a mid-point in our lives? There
is no neatness with mine.

I was about to have perhaps *the* greatest shock of my life;
here in Tokyo.

This was not to do with the shaking foundations of a
marriage relationship. It was not an aftershock of the
reverberation of motherhood; this was to do with *me, my* very
core and *my* very being

In the process of adopting eight day old 'Lotus Blossom,'
lovely Alison Rachel with sticking up hair – I now discovered
at the age of thirty-three, that *I* was adopted!

I was to find out, in the afternoon mail, that my genealogy
was a bit 'squiffy.' I had absolutely no idea, not even the
remotest clue.

So I shall sit and write. Write in review, filling in gaps and
spaces, cutting and pasting emotions, disasters and dreams. I
think a good a place to start is what I shall term, 'childhood and
beyond.'

During the process of adoption, I had to prove to Mr Warren-Knott and the British Embassy that I was a British citizen by birth.

I had always had my short birth certificate, I had used it for university, marriage and employment.

Now, for Alison's adoption procedure, we both needed to prove that we were British citizens by birth.

Instead of asking our parents to send our long birth certificates, I wrote urgently direct to Somerset House.

Less than two weeks later, the awaited documents arrived.

There was Michael's certificate, but as regards to mine, the letter stated that my original could not be sent. All that was enclosed in the letter was the relevant entry in the Adopted Children's Register.

"Idiots," I thought, "useless bureaucrats."

★★★

Then alone in the apartment, I sat down. It hit me with the force of a tidal wave. No, no, this wasn't a mistake. They don't send details like this in error.

I rang Michael at the office.

"I have just had a dreadful shock," I related, "I found out that I am adopted."

"By which organization?" he said, I suppose thinking that I was to embark on some project or other.

"No," I said. "*Adopted.*"

Silence for a moment, then, "we'll talk about it tonight when I get home."

Empathy works with a time line. It was not his greatest feature.

I sat and sat and within a few moments, I *knew*.

I had the overwhelming feeling that if I was adopted as I had read, then the birth mother was my mother's sister, Auntie Dorothy.

It was an illogical, inexplicable but totally overwhelming gut feeling.

★★★

That afternoon I was due to go to my regular Bible Study group.

This was an Interdenominational gathering – differing nationalities – a gathering of anything from ten to twenty women at a time. I loved it.

Not much studying *this* afternoon. I told them of my news as soon as I was through the door.

"Wait a minute," said one, "isn't you first name Dorothy?"

It had never really impacted me, I hadn't really given it much thought but yes it was, "Dorothy Judith."

For the next three days or so, it all felt surreal. Who was I? I had all the family photos I could lay my hands on, spread out on the bed. Who did I look like?

Did my father have an affair with his sister-in-law? Was my father really my birth father? If not, who was the father, if, convinced as I was, Dorothy was the mother?

Events and scenes in such moments overlap. It is a collage of memories, odd and strange. I see myself as a child in the back pew of that cold and draughty Welsh church, the child who thought that the eleventh commandment was 'Thou Shalt Wear a Hat.'

Sitting next to me is my mother, the dominant force, who could lash a person to the mast at four paces, with her tongue.

The one who, it seems, 'did her duty' and sorted out the mess of her younger, pregnant sister.

Was this conjecture?

What happened between these two sisters, if my conclusions were correct and Dorothy was my birth mother? That would then make Iris not my mother as I thought, but my Aunt.

All this was happening simultaneously with Alison's adoption.

It was like flicking between two T.V. channels.

One moment I would be trying to work out all my birth entanglement, and then completing some aspect of hers.

No wonder that prayer, that day, with Pam Pak and Geri Miler about my birth had some sort of impact. My birth had been a less than joyous event for whoever my birth mother was.

★★★

A year later, I was to discover the truth. Alison's adoption was now all completed.

We were back in London; I had gone to Somerset House to be shown my original birth certificate. The procedure meant that I was to be shown it in the presence of a counsellor.

They had refused to send the information while we were in Japan.

There it was:

'Name of Mother: Dorothy May Morgan...

Name of Father: (blank).'

Some weeks later, I am on my own with my mother in the kitchen, my father is at work. I start the inevitable conversation. My counselling training kicks in, "Would you sit down, 'Mam' I have something important to tell you." I tell her simply that I know.

That in the process of adopting Lotus Blossom (Alison's nickname), I find out that I am adopted. I tell her I know that Dorothy is the birth mother, I ask her poignantly in that neat kitchen, "Was my father an American airman?"

Why this came into my mind I have never been quite sure, apart from the fact that Dorothy was a midwife and nursing Sister at a London hospital, I had been told once that she had nursed American airmen!

These are moments when time stops, when those on another shore, the surrounding cloud of witnesses hold their breath and wait for the answer.

It came in sobs which I had never before seen in this tough, organized, strong woman, my mother/aunt.

"No certainly not. Your father was Herbert Walter Rice-Evans."

The secret was disclosed.

I was made, wherever, by a 'Dorothy May Morgan' and a 'Herbert Walter Rice-Evans,' J.P., local squire.

Herbert was certainly *not* an American airman, 'over here and overpaid.' I was not a Yank.

I wanted to scream, to use expletives, to shout out that this was all about me, but no one had ever told *me*. I felt it was like a touch of the Tom Jones, foundling.

★★★

How did it all come about? Where now was this Father Name: (blank), person? How could someone called 'Herbert' have fathered me? I had never seen his picture, but it seems that everyone else in the family had.

It is an odd experience to blissfully write all the facts of one's medical history based on my fighting fit mother; and to write about the medical history of 'David Henry Davies,' reserved man, undertaker, my father of the carpentry shop childhood, and yet to know nil of the medical history of the, never – seen – illusive – Herbert, who had fathered me and walked off of the page.

It was a lot to take in. My mother, after her tears, told me that day in the kitchen how I had come into *her* life. I had not come as an eight day old with sticking up black hair. I had not come with a day's notice.

My story was the material of Hollywood. Pregnant Dorothy tells the world she is changing her job (a midwife and a ward sister in a hospital). She goes to London.

No give away bump, to bring disgrace on the teetotal patriarch Jack, her father. Jack has kept a pub for thirty years, swears like a trooper, but does not let a drop pass his lips.

His wife Rose, my grandmother, is let in on the secret. So are Dorothy's two sisters, Iris and Peggy. The plan is formed.

When the baby is born, my parents, Iris and David, married fifteen years with a ten year old son; they will take and adopt the child.

Off to London goes Dorothy, aged thirty six to deliver me.

Even my passport is inaccurate. I was always told I was born in Skewen, and now I find I am not exotically Welsh, but made my debut in a nursing home in Surrey.

Forget maternal bonding. Bonding? With whom did I bond?

Apparently some nurse friend and colleague of Dorothy's. I was in her care until at five months of age – my mother and aunt come to collect me.

They return back to Wales with a 'Dr. Barnardo's child' as everyone is told. I was by all accounts, sickly looking with a terrible nappy rash.

In the rest of my entire life, I was never to see Auntie Dorothy, *aka* birth mother, on my own. My mother had made it clear that she did not want anyone, to tell me anything!

What I do remember is that before any important event in my life, I would get a long, encouraging letter from Dorothy, and for every birthday I would be given a well-chosen, expensive present.

Each time she looked at me growing up, it was if she studied every small expression, every feature of my face. Now finding out that perhaps I was not who I thought I was, gave me the freedom to invent my own self.

Herbert can become 'exotic, intelligent, convivial Herbert.' I have no photograph to see if I have his eyes or the same mouth. He is wonderfully anonymous and blank. I can make him taller, thinner and debonair. I can invent his likes and dislikes, his skills and aptitudes.

Did he have any interest in what happened to me after he got his 'leg over?'

★★★

Dorothy has long since gone. So has Herbert.

I am told that day, in that kitchen telling of my story, that he had died two years previously, aged seventy eight. He had never married nor had other children.

I was also told that he knew that Iris had adopted me, he had admitted paternity. I was told that my father, David, had made it clear that he wanted nothing from Herbert and certainly no contact.

I was adopted, documents sealed under the law at the time, and that was it.

The story is not finished; it was yet to come full circle.

Twelve years after this conversation in the neat Welsh kitchen, I sit in my Princeton U.S. 'Walk-in' wardrobe, probing the deepest secrets of my life amid the coat hangers and fraying jeans.

I experienced what I can only describe as an overwhelming urge to ring Auntie Dorothy, now in her early eighties; in Wales.

I had never rung her before, certainly not from abroad.

I telephone Dorothy, asking her if she is alone, and in good professional counselling training yet again, asking her to sit down.

Twelve years later, twelve years after I had heard the details in that kitchen, twelve years after I know the story of my adoption.

I tell her that I know she is my birth mother.

She, however, unlike Iris, does not cry. She says slowly, "I always wanted to tell you, but they wouldn't let me. We never thought you would find out. I would never have given you to anyone else, but Iris. I knew she and David would look after you. Do not think badly of me. I want you to forgive me."

After a pause, she asks, "Would you do something for me? Please would you call me 'Mother' — just one time?"

That was something I just could not do.

My mother was my mother.

My mother, Iris, was the one who took me to school, brought me boiled eggs in bed when I was ill, bought me dolls for Christmas and arranged extra tutoring when I struggled with algebra.

I never did see Dorothy on my own.

The following year when we were back in England on home leave, I visited her with my mother. Dorothy, now a frail figure in a nursing home hunched in a wheelchair, who, when I said my name — asked if I was *her* Judith!

Then the words from which film scripts are made.

"I always prayed for you to be a missionary."

So corny, yet, so heart stopping, yet so true.

That is what she said, prayed for me to be a missionary!

To wish me in darkest Africa a la Dr Livingstone, who knows, maybe to assuage the guilt of dumping me on her brother-in-law and sister. They who were seeking to rebuild their lives following the Second World War.

I will never know why she said those words. It was a scene par excellence.

There we were in the nursing home, Dorothy croaking, "I love you."

And my mother screaming out, "Liar!"

★★★

How could such crass intensity have ever made it into the neatly sanitized first draft of my memoirs?

91

Over the years I have had many moments of reflection.

Did Dorothy, a trained midwife who had dealt with abortions in the days of coat hangers and gin, ever try to put an end to little old me?

If that was the case, well, it didn't work and I am glad. I am glad that an eighteen year old Japanese girl went full term and decided adoption to a foreign couple.

Life is full of intersections.

My life intersected dramatically with that "Alison Rachel Thomas." I adopt a Japanese baby girl, darling Lotus Blossom with sticking up hair, and in the middle of the process, my own adoption is uncovered!

"We never thought you would find out."

Those were my mother's words, the documents had been sealed, the issue closed and because of the process of adopting Alison, I had received the most impacting news of my life.

I probably would never have had the need to use a long birth certificate.

What did this event termed adoption mean for those involved? I had adopted a child, I had cried when I thought of what Alison's mother had gone through in her decision.

Now I find out that I was adopted.

Dorothy had, throughout all the years, the pain and joy of living about fifteen minutes from my parents, seeing me grow and yet not being able to tell me.

She had, however, the satisfaction of knowing that I had turned out 'tidily.'

I think I will leave the planet without ever discovering about Herbert Walter, father non-extraordinaire.

All Dorothy told me in that Princeton walk-in wardrobe conversation that day was that he had auburn hair, was a lovely man and that she would love him till the day she died. Who knows, maybe that was her Hollywood story.

Maybe that was more palatable than the truth, I guess, that I will never know.

QUESTIONS:

This chapter covers some deep and poignant issues.

How would you cope with "untidiness in your family tree?"

Have you already had to do this?

What are some of the issues that puzzle you as you consider your own family past?

The author speaks of discovering the secret of her adoption.

How are secrets dealt with in your family?

The issue of abortion is raised. How do you feel about this?

Chapter Twelve

FLOWER POWER AND JESS

Adoption completed. Alison Rachel Thomas leaves Japan on her Japanese passport. We enter Dubai en route and she has a six day Japanese Businessman's Visa stamped in it.

There are no visas for Japanese babies passing through Dubai with Welsh parents, (another Alison precedent, also mentioned in her father's speech on her wedding day).

Our assignment in Japan is complete. Michael, I and our gorgeous six month old daughter are now ready to move to the next assignment – San Francisco.

There we are, two adults and a baby with now tamed hair, pushing her stroller up and down the good old streets of San Francisco.

'Haight Ashbury,' wild, wild California. Wild and decadent 'bath houses.' San Francisco of the early eighties, pre AIDS, in your face-gay San Francisco.

Our apartment was near Fisherman's Wharf, a gated community from which Michael could walk to work.

I spent my days walking with Alison through parks and up and down the streets. We were an anomaly, but anything went in those days.

We passed happy couples holding hands and caressing,

men with men, women with women, not quite 'tidy' like South Wales.

Our first Christmas in San Francisco was rapidly approaching and with Alison a toddler, there should have been an infectious enthusiasm with its coming. But I didn't want to write cards, nor put out any decorations. It all seemed an effort.

Before I seemed to know it, New Year came, and I just couldn't be bothered. My body seemed to be on one of its usual halts, familiar to me each time we moved. The days passed. I felt sluggish.

★★★

We had a wonderful neighbour in the apartment below. Laura had a seven year old boy, if there were special occasions to attend, we often shared baby-sitting. As she listened to me describe my lethargy, she sipped her coffee, looked at me and said, "Come on, have a pregnancy test. I know a clinic, near Chinatown, instant results, we'll go there tomorrow."

Laura was newly pregnant with her second child, and I put this statement down to over enthusiasm with her condition. She had motherhood on her mind, no doubt.

My menstruation on the other hand seemed to take a vacation every time we moved. It would just stop. With ears deaf to my protestation that it was a waste of time, she said, "I'll pick you up at ten. We will take Alison with us. You have the test, and then we will all go out for a nice lunch together."

The clinic was in downtown Chinatown, a Chinatown that was *very* Chinese. We stood out amid the 'kanji' and red painted signs.

Looking back on events, I remember lots of young girls in the clinic's bare waiting room. I recall that on the form there were phrases which stated that if you were 'sixteen' and pregnant you could apply for further counselling. You could, with that euphemism, 'get further advice.'

I duly filled in the paperwork, and gave the ubiquitous sample bottle. Then came the twenty minutes wait for the result.

I was called into another room by a diminutive, Chinese woman, in an overly large white coat.

She told me solemnly to sit down. With a tone and facial expression that seemed appropriate to an approaching world disaster, she sighed deeply and said, "It's positive."

There are times when my brain seems to go into overdrive. The words were hardly out of her Chinese mouth before I said, "Do it again!"

I am one hundred per cent sure that I must have been the only one in that clinic that day, or if ever, who then shouted, "Hooray!"

I told her that after eleven years, of being told that we couldn't have children, of eleven years with not even a hint of conception, this was "something else."

Then she shouted, "Hooray, I'll do it again!"

The count-on-one-hand moments of intimacy in my marriage, it must have been next in terms of a miraculous event, to Angel Gabriel's assignment.

★★★

When I re-joined Laura in the waiting room, she said, "O.K. let's go," and bending down, she began to button Alison's coat. She was almost out of the door, when I said, "Laura, it was positive."

Then she swung around at speed, whirling a startled Alison in tow, and exclaimed in a gasp, "Get them to do it again!"

No mobile phone days then, we went off in shock for our planned meal at the Mexican restaurant. Alison was just over a year old, far beyond her remembering and comprehension.

We rang Michael at the office. He was in a meeting. He called back later. "I had the test," I said slowly.

"You are not too disappointed are you?"

Laura, hearing this could hardly suppress a giggle.

"No," I said solemnly, "it was positive."

Silence at the end of the telephone. Then the response that was to become the mantra, "Get them to do it again."

In the next few weeks, I think I broke the record for pregnancy tests.

To say that it was a shock to us was the understatement of all time.

★★★

The next day, I, who had thought this pregnancy thing isn't too bad, I, who the previous day had munched through enchiladas, tostadas and re-fried beans, was hit with all the intensity of morning sickness – and afternoon and evening sickness!

It was now as if my body was really going to show me that I was pregnant. Just to look at meat. Let alone cook it. Would send me pale and shuffling off to the nearest bathroom.

For six months (I was some weeks along) I was never to venture out unless my pockets were stuffed with crackers, unable to think or want food in all its variety. They would keep me going between the bouts of finding the nearest toilet.

Yet, I grew, I puffed out, it was indeed happening. Gradually my body got the message and settled down.

Laura and I went to the same gynaecologist and we would be having our babies within just a few weeks of each other.

All my training for natural childbirth would go by the board and twenty three weary hours later, Jessica Elizabeth Thomas, the only American at that time in the family, entered the world in the presence of two very weary parents.

We had gone from no children to two children in twenty one months. It was as if one miracle was not enough, this was an encore by a mega-merciful and loving God.

Michael and I had in our life journey together gone through an adoption and a birth, we were above all parents, loving and doting. We had two little girls. Both were destined to be dressed in Welsh costume every St David's Day.

★★★

San Francisco became for me a period of reassessment.

It seemed to encapsulate two worlds. One of intense activity, as I dealt with two small children; and the other, was a feeling, of spiritual dryness.

These wonderful events had happened – but in the day to day. I felt as if God had put me on a shelf and walked away, I felt blessed, no question, yet it was a deep time, it was a growing, dark-in-the-earth time.

San Francisco was a strange city and was not one geared to families. We were there almost fifteen months, and now, once again, we were preparing for our next assignment.

Long distance, far away New Zealand.

QUESTIONS:

The author speaks of the miracle of birth.

What has been your experience of this?

The author writes of two important and enduring women friends in her life.

How important are such friendships in your life?

The author writes of a spiritual barrenness – of feeling 'left on the shelf and God walking away'

Have you ever had a similar experience?

Chapter Thirteen

KIWI CHICKENS AND CEREAL BLOSSOM

We are now parents of two, one with black hair and one with flaming Titian red. They are nicknamed Lotus Blossom and Apple Blossom by my mother.

We leave for the next assignment in New Zealand. We get on the plane, half our luggage consisting of diapers and baby bottles, and every item necessary to keep small persons amused for the twenty hour plus journey. Our eventual destination will be New Plymouth, North Island, and the area we would fondly call "Nappy Valley."

What strange impressions various countries conjure up in the mind. When Michael told me that our next assignment would be New Zealand my immediate reaction was to think of legs of lamb and that wonderful New Zealand butter that we would often buy.

New Zealand was to prove a country of breath-taking beauty, especially the South Island with its lakes of incomparable azure and turquoise, the renowned fiord landscape of Queenstown and Milford Sound. No postcards seem to do it justice.

Mount Taranaki, a double for familiar Mt. Fuji, dominated the area in which we lived.

We lived in a brand new spacious, company house, with the others on the project. Many were Americans. This was a totally different experience for all of us.

New Zealand had something like ten sheep for every person! Seeing them contentedly munching in the fields would remind us nostalgically of Wales.

Babies in strollers would sit on sheepskins, they would loll in their cribs on sheepskins, you would sit on sheepskin covers in your car, and at home you would walk in sheepskin slippers, and yes, on a cold day you would brave the elements in a sheepskin hat and coat!

There was the incongruity of the southern hemisphere, where December would be one of the hottest months, and Christmas dinner would be a barbecue with a visit to the pool afterwards. This was New Zealand. I am afraid, at that time in my life, a lot of it was wasted on me.

It was 'outdoorsy,' I was not.

★★★

The area of company houses provided a safe haven for the growing families, it was a happy time. It was a great place to bring up children, we did activities as a community, and the children were never lost for playmates.

It was family time; one of the neighbouring Americans had a trampoline. How the brains of our offspring were not totally scrambled with all this bouncing about, I do not know.

New Zealand was the complete opposite of swinging San Francisco. We used to joke that New Zealand closed on a Friday and opened again on a Monday.

It was so different from California life where we had spent nearly two years. New Zealand was a 'no nonsense place.' a straightforward place, a 'tidy' place. The Maori culture was fascinating, most of the Maoris being found in the North Island.

Their carvings reminded me of Polynesia; it was not that long ago that New Zealand had been a pioneer country.

The children went to kindergarten and flourished. I thought back to my working life, my career in human resources and training. On the two days that the Alison and Jessica would be in kindergarten, what would I do? I was still completing endless Theological correspondence courses and enjoying every minute of it.

There was also something else available which would combine the both aspects of Industry *and* Theology.

★★★

New Zealand had a system of Industrial Chaplains. It was administered by an organization called ITIM. – Interfaith Trade and Industry Mission. I had the industrial background, I had the theological training. I applied, was interviewed, vetted and approved. I was rearing to go.

There were a variety of available companies.

Yes, I knew about them; yes, an insurance office, that sounded good, yes, a department store, excellent, I had experience of that – and then there was a chicken factory – UGH!

It was a no-brainer, of course, as to which location I would get sent.

I, who, as a teenager had looked with disdain on uncooked meat, I, who could easily end up a vegetarian, was sent to 'Tegel Chickens,' where 54,000 chickens *per day* came in squawking and went out at the end of it boxed and frozen !

How much more pleasant, I reflected to walk around a department store, trying the cosmetic samples and looking at the latest acquisitions on the lingerie section, than to be in Wellington boots, a white coat and a hard hat helmet, sloshing with the chickens!

Slosh about I did, sloshing twice a week, looking as if I had come off the moon shuttle. It was here, however, amid chicken entrails that the gospel came to life.

★★★

"The Industrial Chaplain," the pamphlet states, "meets all levels of staff, and is there with the agreement of both management and unions, but is independent of both." As well as offering his or her own help and counsel, the chaplain is trained to put a person in touch with a wide range of people both in the workplace and the community, such as marriage guidance, or a family counsellor etc.

The chaplain seeks to find the right help, but is also free to share what the Christian faith is about to anyone who wants to know – I was one! A trained, enthusiastic chaplain – but I still had to deal with the chickens!

The thought of entering the shed where the chickens were being killed, churned my stomach.

Outside, the birds were squawking in their cages, and their faces seemed more cartoon-like by the second.

How on earth did I find myself here?

However, the desire to be a "good chaplain" overcame me. I thought of the Maori girl who worked alone in the shed.

I took the deepest breath I think I have ever taken, and in I went.

By some tremendous effort, I felt as if I was scuba diving. "Do not breathe in." I said to myself, "Pace your breathing, expel only."

I tried to talk to her without my eyes straying an inch to the right, nor to the left, in order to avoid seeing some horrible sight which I knew I would never be able to handle. Her arm, as we talked, would occasionally move across in a quick, clean movement, and I groaned inwardly as my always fertile imagination worked overtime.

She was slitting the throats of chirpy chickens.

My air intake was running out. I had managed to talk for some minutes it seemed, without inhaling. Mission accomplished! I bade her farewell and left the shed. I felt like a church martyr.

★★★

The other areas in the factory were only fractionally more pleasant.

As I talked to the men and women who worked there, chickens in various stages of portioning would fly past on overhead conveyor belts.

They were surreal, 'Daliesque.'

My favourite section was the chicken liver one. Not without cost, I had to forego the pleasure of eating it for years – for obvious reasons – I knew how it was made.

Granny, the supervisor of that section was a large Maori woman whose husband was dying of cancer...

She did not want her husband told by the doctors of the seriousness of his illness. The strain of keeping up the pretence that "all was well" was tearing her apart.

"Do you honestly believe, Judith, that there is life after this one?" she would ask, and in my way, not from any personal experience, I would try to answer her.

The weeks passed, and each week I saw her face showed increasing pain.

Then it was over. A burden lifted, he had died...

Granny took a long leave of absence and she went to England, yet, I have often thought of our conversations together.

Less than two years later, I was to have the same conversation with my mother about my father. This time the pain would be on her face.

★★★

There I was, an industrial chaplain, mother of Alison and Jessica, double stroller pusher and in my quiet moments, I pondered the possibility that maybe, just maybe, lightning *would* strike a third time.

I was thirty seven and I wanted to have another child.

Michael and I talked and it was not about adoption. It was about good old natural means.

I needed co-operation in the matter and the method. He was open to the possibility. It was to be considered.

It is amazing but those 'count on the fingers of one hand moments' moved yet another gear in heaven and soon I was a *pregnant*, industrial chaplain in a hard hat.

The smell of chickens and morning sickness do not go well. I finished my chicken assignment and bade farewell to my feathered friends.

I would not have to hear another joke, about ministering – 'on a wing and a prayer.'

The months of the pregnancy went past without incident and I felt as if my Welsh body had now got the hang of this whole pregnancy thing. No natural childbirth moments now in the hospital where I was to give birth but with good old NZ 'gas and air.'

I floated into delivery and a few hours later, when a slimy little person was laid on my stomach, I exclaimed,

"It's a little boy!"

Owen Philip Thomas had joined the group.

This time, a less than weary father took him in his arms.

We were now a family of five, a black haired, a red haired and a blonde, one born Tokyo, one born San Francisco and now one born New Zealand. We had gone from zero to this in an unbelievably short time. As a toddler he would love to enjoy bowls of cereal – now we were complete – Lotus Blossom, Apple Blossom and an obscurely named Cereal Blossom!

Three different passports now and horrendous immigration details to be completed on each following trip, wherever that next assignment would be!

QUESTIONS:

What do you think of the concept of an industrial chaplain?

Think of some of the situations in your work experience where, an industrial chaplain might have been helpful.

The author is now mother of three children.

How do you think moving around the world affects children and families?

What would be your concerns?

Have you ever relocated with your family?

Was it a positive experience?

Chapter Fourteen

BATIK BATTLES

Our time in New Zealand was drawing to a close. It was time to say goodbye, to chicken memories; and to say goodbye to our time in wonderful Happy Nappy Valley.

Goodbye sheep. Hello 'Al Capone' country.

Next we would be back to the States to Joliet, Illinois, 'Mafia Joliet.' Michael was to be the refinery Project Manager. It was the coldest place I have ever lived, the children walked around like a family of Michelin midgets, forever in insulated suits and coats. I was frozen. I was putting the last picture on the wall of our rented house when I got a phone call from Michael.

"I have been offered an assignment in Indonesia. Mobil wants me there as Systems Engineering Manager on a new, ground breaking project. How do you feel about our moving there?"

It was a superfluous question. My little Welsh heart jumps at the thought of confronting new cultures. It was blatantly obvious to me. Hot and wonderful, inscrutable Far East versus cold Mafioso Illinois!

My bags were mentally packed.

★★★

In these months, what was happening in the marriage? Busy with three, very different, very busy children and enjoying all that brings, the thought of my marriage relationship had long been shelved. I was exhausted at night and days were crammed with activity.

The days of solitary matrimony passed quickly and we were both totally occupied. I was absorbed in out-of-one's mind motherhood; he was entrenched in his work. Now there would be the excitement of another project, another move. I couldn't wait for the exhilaration of it all.

The adrenalin was already pumping! I knew Michael was looking forward to the challenge of the project in Jakarta. He loved his job and was good at it.

"We are going to Indonesia! Where exactly is that?"

I went off hurriedly searching for the well-worn atlas. Prior to our move to Japan, at least I had some preconceived ideas of the country, no matter how inadequate these were, but of Indonesia I knew nothing.

I had heard of that tropical paradise Bali, and as we poured over the maps, I had a shock to realise that this was one of the thousands of islands which make up the Indonesian archipelago. Being an 'international jetsetter' of sorts has done wonderful things for my knowledge of geography.

In the days following, I would hunt frantically among my old National Geographics, and I would spend ages at the library copying everything I could find on this far away country.

I emerged a week later with the following facts which I would rattle off to all and sundry, "Indonesia lies between the two continents, the Asian mainland, and Australia, and is served by two vast oceans, the Pacific and the Indian Ocean. Stretching across some three thousand miles plus, Indonesia comprises of five main islands, Java being the most fertile, and supporting some 60% of the population.

Sumatra is the third largest of the Indonesian islands with approximately one fourth of the country's total land area. Indonesia had then a population of about one hundred and fifty million people, and the number of languages and dialects spoken is classified as anything between 250 and 400."

Those facts I had memorized and could recite them parrot-fashion, but I would have a field day trying to absorb the language and grammar!

★★★

We were to be located first in Java then Sumatra, areas where hepatitis, malaria and indeed leprosy were still rampant. We were to spend the project assignment in two locations first in Jakarta and then in Lhokseumawe, Aceh province in the north. Besides all the impressive facts I rattled off, I was also to learn in my nearly five years in the country, that a kitchen might be shared with cockroaches and little lizards called '*cik caks.'*

I would discover the necessity of having household help in this over-powering humid climate. Humidity means a rapid turnover in men's socks – whether worn out, or 'borrowed' by the household help! I also learned that all things which may have been previously dry cleaned will be washed, no matter what. Shrinkage and colour-run are not part of the equation.

I was to be confronted by the first of my many ethical decisions. I baulked at the thought of having servants. When we arrived in Jakarta, I firmly resolved that I would do things myself. To have household help, servants, smacked to me of colonial days, to someone new to the country like me, it seemed like modern day slavery.

In a city like Jakarta, which sees moisture dripping down the walls, which is on the Equator and is so humid that you end up changing your clothes three or four times a day, my ethical dilemma lasted three exhausted days. My ethical dilemma did not withstand the fact that clothes were an 'oh so creaseable cotton' and floors were a 'white, needing to be washed daily, shiny marble' – I succumbed,

"Servants. Servants yes please," I begged.

They were critical, essential, vitally needed – I knew it in my soul – that plus the fact that the washing machine was outdated, and the iron seemed to have a will of its own. How else would the umpteen-times-plus daily washing of the floors, the disinfecting of the vegetables and the lettuce get done? If we were not all to be struck down with those parasites and diseases, servants it would be. Not least of all they would be forefront warriors in getting rid of this super strain of cockroaches, who seemed determine to win against all odds! Wonder Woman, I was not!

"Servants. Servants yes please!"

There was now not even a dilemma. I would employ – Sudar, Siti and Harianti – ethically. By my employing them, I reasoned, it would give them an income, help them. I could not wait. Like 'Topsy,' the decision to employ staff was forced to expand. I ended up overflowing with household help.

Like every other family on the project we were told by the Company that we must employ other workers. We must employ two watchmen – one for the day, the other for the night, we were also required to employ a driver as we were not allowed to drive in Indonesia.

We had a huge garden and a swimming pool in this colonial style home. I had thought maybe I could dabble in the work of the garden, "That would be fine," I was told, as long as I knew which plants were deadly, which caused a blistering rash and which attracted rats.

We made the ethical decision to employ a gardener!

★★★

In the evenings, our night watchman, Supardi, would sit in the still blistering heat of the evening, proudly wearing a woollen balaclava. He was a strict Muslim, and rigidly observed prayer time. He had been the house 'security force' for twelve years. He would patrol the grounds with great fervour.

The house was surrounded by an eight foot wall with vicious barbed wire on top. We carefully avoided showing such details as this in the photographs to Welsh relatives back home.

On the hottest of tropical nights, woollen balaclava clad, he would sit happily in his watchman hut. In the early days of our assignment, as he passed the kitchen window before going on duty, I would greet him with "Good Evening Supardi."

I always wondered why, when I said this, he had a miffed expression and would go back out through the gate again. I later found out why. He was a *strict* Muslim and he had just prepared himself for prayer. Talking to a woman made him unclean. So he had to start the washing process all over again.

We all had a lot to learn.

★★★

Japan had been a land of affluence, now we were in a country whose per capita income is something like five hundred dollars a year, in a city of something like eight million people, where the contrasts between the very wealthy and the very poor affront you sharply.

A box of 'Western' cereal in the super-market was as often as much, as someone working in the fields would earn in one day. 'Cereal Blossom' would have to be in withdrawal.

Still sending off my theological correspondence courses, these issues of plenty amid poverty, lavishness amid extreme want, were all things with which I wrestled on a daily basis. The children were small, Owen not two years old, keeping all of us healthy was a major issue.

We were looked after by an excellent company doctor, and a comprehensive medical scheme, whereas the vast majority of Indonesians dreaded sickness, and the poverty and distress that it might bring. If a member of their family became ill, they risked dying needlessly as affording proper medical treatment was often impossible.

Ours was a strange expat existence.

To the average Indonesian, every Westerner they met was, by definition, a Christian. It was an assumption that they made. I wondered how they judged those Western men who, night after night, were propping up bars in the red light districts. They were often the prey of 'white hunters,' the girls who saw them and other foreigners, as a meal ticket out.

★★★

Siti, our cook, was a wonderful woman, with poise and dignity. In any other society she would have been a well-educated woman in her own right, with much to contribute. As it was, with lack of educational opportunity, she would probably be a servant all her life.

Once, when she was desperately ill, we suspected her appendix was on the point of bursting. As I sat with her in her room, all barriers of race, religion, culture, all disappeared. We were two women and I respected her. It saddened me to see how the Jakarta hospital, where she was immediately sent with suspected imminent peritonitis, treated the servant class.

At three in the morning in the pouring monsoon rain, her husband was sent out to get the medicine the hospital did not have in stock. If I had needed medicine I would have been given it immediately. I was a white expat.

Living in Indonesia for all those years, I struggled to show courtesy to others in every situation, and above all "to show love."

★★★

There were occasions when this was strained to the limit and the 'fuse episode' was one of them.

It was one of those expat incidences abroad which were to be priceless – told and retold later at endless dinner parties.

This was how it went. The electricity in the house went off, a not unusual occurrence. It was a fact of Jakarta life – there would be hours of power cuts when everything would stop and then come mysteriously back on. I knew, from past experience it was a fuse in the large box outside the front gate. I followed the procedure and called the company's trouble-shooter maintenance department.

For some unknown reason, the trouble-shooter maintenance department always arrived in multiples of three. Later, a speedy two and a half hours later, they were finally there. The concept of time is very flexible in the tropics. "*Belum,*" they say – "Not yet!"

Out we all trooped to the fuse box. The three Indonesian musketeers stood behind me as I opened wide the door of the box to show them the offending problem. The next moment, it was like some strange, choreographed dance – *they* all seemed to jump up, do a kind of twist and ended up paces behind me.

Still standing at the open box, I tried to work out if the Indonesian word they were saying repeatedly was one I knew. By this time, my vocabulary was quite extensive, but I didn't recognize this particular one. I left them and trundled off to the house returning with my faithful dictionary. They repeated it; they were repeating it many times, in fact. I slowly looked it up.

God is merciful indeed – there was a built-in time-delay from my hearing the word, and then finding its meaning – "*Cobra.*"

King Cobra was there, for all to see – except me. King Cobra, happy snake that he was – among our fuses! Then we ALL jumped back!!

★★★

It was typical of the phenomenon that was Jakarta – a myriad of street sights.

There were two dead bodies outside the gate one day, the result of a car accident. Then there was the enormous pile of bricks that appeared and disappeared. There would be men on bicycles with huge piles of bananas, so enormous that you wondered how they could keep their balance. It was all a world of colours, sounds and indescribable smells.

It was in Jakarta that I ate enough rice and '*chabe,*' (hot spicy peppers) to last me a life time. The smells of the city were just that – indescribable. There was the infamous '*durian,*' which looked like a small brown landmine. There were the smells of the rotting vegetables, the open sewers, everything mingled – the pineapples, the other exotic fruit, the odour of coconuts, it was sensory overload.

Amid all this, the children managed to get educated. Alison and Jessica went to the American school of Jakarta, Owen to a nearby expat kindergarten. They grew, smothered with sunscreen and eating their disinfected vegetables. They played on the lawn in their sandals avoiding passing parasites and poisonous plants!

***

Each day, Warsiman our driver would weave skilfully in and out of traffic. The company insisted we employ a driver for the practical reason that if any of its staff had an accident in Indonesia, it would automatically be deemed that they were guilty, by reason of the fact that, 'they were in the country to start with!'

The rule of the road seemed to be 'small give way to big', and we were at the mercy of orange '*bajais*,' three-wheeled motorised vehicles which propelled themselves menacingly towards you, missing you only by inches it seemed.

We would pass '*becaks*' a kind of updated rickshaw, where the driver on his bicycle would operate from behind. We would pass whole families on motorbikes – father first, then balanced somewhere in between the parents, would be two or three toddlers. Mother was perched precariously, but modestly at the rear, side-saddle.

***

It was here on the street where horns seemed to be used at every opportunity, here amid the buzz, throb and rhythm of Jakarta streets, that I saw *her*. I realised that at no matter what time of day we passed she was always at the same spot.

As our car moved into the outside lane, I could see her clearly. She was dressed in a traditional batik '*sarung*,' a wrap-around skirt, whose colours had long since gone. At her side was a roll of cloth, like a thin carpet. In the heat of the tropical day, I wondered how on earth she managed.

Sometimes, piled on her head was a bundle of brown cloth, which looked as if she had tried to make some elaborate kind of turban that had gone wrong. Her hair was matted into a long plait.

The thing that completely astonished me was the length of her nails, unbelievably long. I remember seeing a photo of ones just like that once, in the Guinness Book of Records. They literally spiralled helter-skelter about six inches from her finger tops.

Warsiman, agreed that she probably lived exactly where she stood – on that very spot. We had not seen her beg, there was no bowl at her side. She was so very different from the beggars who rushed at our car as we stopped at the traffic lights near the mosque. They would carry forlorn babies, who I later discovered were rented per day for this very purpose (and not always the same babies). She was on my mind more and more. I asked Siti to prepare some hot noodles, chicken and some rice.

Off I went in a self-congratulatory mood, like a Welsh angel of mercy.

The car stopped, there she was, I risked life and limb to dodge cars which seemed to come at me from every direction. I stood in front of her, and nervously thrust the containers into her hands. I was totally unprepared for the reaction. That 'catonic' look of hopelessness that I had seen time after time as we passed changed. She smiled. I had never for once thought that a smile would be her reaction.

Then she said in a slow, distinct voice, "Thank You."

As I shut the car door, Warsiman and I saw her give the 'thumbs-up' sign. From that point on, our meetings became a daily occurrence. I looked forward to seeing her – the two thumbs up, waving them around madly.

Of all the partings on our assignments, that was one of the saddest.

★★★

It was time to finish in Jakarta, and to move to the project site of Lhokseumawe, North Sumatra. Lhokseumawe was a multi-billion dollar project, designed to tap a deposit of natural gas. The site seemed to be a strange anomaly, to the surrounding rice paddies, and grazing bullocks. Strange indeed, to put a modern gas refining plant there.

The special province of Aceh was one of the first points of contact in Indonesia of Islam. The area had a fierce reputation. It was a very 'difficult' place.

Once there, as a family we once again slipped into 'settling in' mode. The children went to a Company school in the compound. There were also medical facilities there and a clubhouse.

Shopping in the commissary and outside became a somewhat thrilling and taxing event. This time, the basic food necessities, (basic by Western standards!) were not always available. When they were available there would be great rejoicing. We would have 'Mayonnaise Arrival' parties.

Many of the project wives, mainly from Texas, would talk with tears in their eyes, of how they missed Gatorade and Twinkies. The fact that most things when they did arrive were months over the date stamp seemed to lose importance. That they were *there* that was all that mattered. They were *there,* to be loved and cherished.

The little things I so valued vanished evaporated. I missed being able to go to bookshops. I missed meeting with my friends from outside the company, I missed just being able to 'get somewhere.'

As foreigners we were tolerated. We were necessary at the refinery. We did not have to be made welcome.

★★★

Every morning, after the children had gone on the school bus, I would go to Laura's. Hers was another project family. I would walk in at the same time as two loudly meowing cats. I reflected that if I had been Mrs Noah, those two would definitely not have made it into the Ark.

Laura and I would have a coffee then we would pray. Sometimes our other friend Lorraine would join us. We prayed for our marriages, we prayed for our husbands, we prayed for our children, we prayed amid interruptions from all sides, from window cleaners, from people wanting to paint, from people wanting to sell batik, from people selling fish... the list was endless – but in those moments I felt a closeness to God in a way that is hard to reproduce.

Here in the frustrations of life in Sumatra. I felt that God cared about the small things. He cared that Jessica sucked her thumb, or that Timothy and Owen were not good sleepers, or that Jon needed to learn English quickly. We prayed about everything. We prayed for the missionaries who came to hold the camp services in the video room, we prayed with words and without words. We prayed by name for the entire household staff, and for our families back home. There were days when we cried. There were days when we felt the oppression of it all – the heat and the enclosure.

We felt the oppression of living in this province of remote Aceh. Some days it seemed that our prayers bounced back at us but we persevered. If we couldn't meet for those twenty or so minutes, then we would telephone each other and pray long distance. I wonder what Ijah or Yunidar, our house help, thought as they heard us. They understood sufficient English to understand. It all seemed a stark contrast to the ritual prayer around us. Their call to worship seemed so far removed from our garbled words, amid two meowing cats.

★★★

My time in Lhokseumawe, North Sumatra would be challenging. My values and my commitment would be continuously in front of me, confronting me. I met people for whom their faith had meant the loss of everything and yet there was a deep joy about them. I had seen and met people whose suffering was beyond my comprehension.

There were the lepers of the village of 'Blang Me' in Aceh, and there were the Cambodian refugees I visited at their camp in Jakarta. What they had endured was all outside my range of experience. I often reflected that it was only location of birth that meant their lives were determined one way, and mine another.

It was with Laura that I visited the Cambodian refugee camp in Jakarta. It looked like an open prison; the residents for the most part had fled from the Khmer Rouge. Our trip had been planned for months, we flew down from Sumatra.

Whether it was the heat, the food, the excitement or the tension, who knows, but as soon as I got there, I felt *sick*.

Here we were waiting to be shown around, to have the opportunity to meet some of the residents and all I wanted to do was to throw up. I suppose I had grand ideas of going there as a kind of Lady Bountiful, seeing myself as in some way different. Now I just wanted to vomit. I was on the point of just this when I managed to quickly say the word for 'toilet.'

'Toilet' – one of the Cambodian ladies rushed me off to a shed. The stench did it. The buzzing black flies did it, the hole in the ground and seeing its contents did it. I vomited and vomited and vomited. I felt her hand gently rubbing my back. "Good," she said. She took a cloth from somewhere and wiped my head.

It was some days later speaking to another friend who had spent time at the camp writing down the various stories, that I discovered that my Cambodian angel of mercy had witnessed her husband and four children being hacked to death by machetes, before her eyes, by the Khmer Rouge. I was humbled. Circumstances can break us, or we can, by God's grace, still find within a human, compassion for others.

★★★

I saw that same compassion again in Indonesia. This time it was on the island of Sumatra. It is a compassion that transcends boundaries.

Sue was an Australian who had been a district nurse in Adelaide. She was also on the project with her family but had already been some years in Lhokseumawe already. She visited a leper village monthly on the outskirts of the town. One day, I went with her.

Leprosy for me had been something I wrote about in my theology essays. It was certainly never something that I had really ever imagined I would confront. For me it was Old and New Testament stuff, never the experience of the twenty first century. I was to find out otherwise.

Forty nine families were there in the leper village of Blang Me. They were living in forced and deliberate isolation. Food would be brought to them or they would go to the outskirts of the town, never closer, to collect it.

The babies born to the families of Blang Me were not born with the disease of leprosy. For these babies and their immature immune systems to be in daily contact with infected parents, meant there was a great likelihood of their catching it. It was, however, a treatable disease, treatable by a course of expensive medication which had to be strictly administered. I felt sick at the sight of some of the running sores, the fingerless hands and the stumps that were feet around me at Blang Me. One of the local charity projects sponsored by the Company was the making of basic coverings, so-called 'shoes' for these often putrid limbs.

We had spent a couple of hours in the heat and the squalor. As we left, Sue shook the hand of the head man of the village. I saw his face. He beamed. He radiated. He came alive. I looked down and saw his hand. It was deformed, missing joints and there were pus-filled sores.

We left.

Outside the village we stopped, she went to the back of the jeep, got a box out and spent the next twenty minutes disinfecting her hands, scrubbing them, washing them meticulously, over and over.

"It took me two years to do that," she said, "but you saw what it meant to him." Yes, I had. Never again was I to feel the same about the lines in Scripture where I read, "And Jesus touched the lepers."

Of all the countries I have lived, I have no desire to return to Indonesia. Not to Bali, and not to Aceh in the north.

★★★

When news of the Tsunami was broadcast I realized that it had affected the town of Lhokseumawe, where I had shopped, where I had lived and where I had brought up the children. Now, the town had been used as a make-shift morgue for the dead. I had sat in those shops, talked to Rusli, bought fabric and haggled for gold.

It had been the most difficult place of all the assignments. I did not miss it. The Western technology was needed and wanted there, but the people – the foreigners that brought it – were not.

Strictly Islamic as a country, it was my first introduction to fanaticism.

Going back to the States after four and a half years in Indonesia, two and a half of them in Aceh was to be a welcome relief. It was the lifestyle it seemed to me, of the British Raj, albeit in this former Dutch colony.

In the master bedroom in Jakarta, there had been a panic button next to the bed. If pressed it would have brought down immediately a protective cage.

A few years before, in the Anglican Church in Jakarta, the priest had been stabbed to death together with his Indonesian night watchman.

Goodbye to cobras, goodbye to leper villages, goodbye paddy fields, goodbye to the Spice Islands.

QUESTIONS:

What ethical issues did you feel were raised by living as an expat in a poor country?

How do you think you would adjust?

What have been some of the situations where you have been aware of the impact of a different religion?

In reading the description of the woman in Jakarta Street or the author's experience in the leper village, what does it say to you of our human ability to show compassion?

Chapter Fifteen

ROBERT WOOD AND REAVILLE

Goodbye cockroaches, goodbye snakes and goodbye to Lhokseumawe.

We are back on home territory. Back, to our lovely home in Pennington, New Jersey. Back, to Ivy League Princeton. Back, to stability. Back to normality and a never-ending supply of mayonnaise, cream cheese, one hundred plus types of cereal and all the food in between. All that had been objects of our Indonesian hallucinations.

"How long do you think we will be here?" I ask,

"At least three years," he answers.

This is it. I am determined to go to full time theological study at Princeton Seminary. There is no opposition. It is the right moment. I have his full support.

I apply for the full time, three years, Master of Divinity degree and I am accepted. After waiting for so long, years to formalize my theological plans, I start at prestigious Princeton Seminary. I also began the process of the long road to ordination; we would see where it would lead.

During this time, Michael was to be travelling abroad with his project work up to two hundred and thirty days of the year. He was gone usually a month or six weeks at a time.

Capable as I was in running the home in his absence, he knew that I needed a focus to nourish me during that time. We had our separate existences in many ways, and when he was home there was the matter of taking the children to their various sport activities, or attending school parent meetings. We were human taxis and sport watchers.

It was one of my happiest periods. I soaked up the studies like an academic sponge. I got the children to bed early enough so that I could begin studying the Hebrew I needed for ordination. It was torture. For my New Testament Greek, also a requirement for ordination, I had private tuition from a Texan doctoral student. Who said that St Paul didn't speak with a Houston drawl!

★★★

At home, I had introduced what the children called, "Bible Time." Various toys and stuffed animals took significant parts as we acted out the familiar Bible tales. These toys would be the required Philistines, Edomites, Amalekites or any other 'ites' needed.

In the story of Hezekiah, the floor was strewn with them, representing the slain Assyrian army. I recall the visit of the Queen of Sheba to King Solomon, Owen sat majestically on the toy box, his plastic gladiator helmet perched rakishly to one side, denoting kingship. Jessica was in another corner, performing some complicated ballet steps which she felt appropriate to the occasion. Alison of Sheba approached, an old cotton kimono covered her nightdress completely; she did a little hop every so often so as not to fall over it. She

132

approaches the king Solomon who is having a lot of trouble keeping the hat from his eyes.

"0'Mighty Lordship," says Lotus Blossom in her loudest voice, "we know you have wisdom. Why did the chicken cross the road? What did the letter say to the stamp?"

I suppose for her that came under the heading of modern exegesis.

They were busy, busy days. I studied while the children were at school, I was always home when they came bursting through the door with their back packs, eager to tell me about the day. At night, their homework finished, I started mine.

★★★

The three years of the M. Div. degree went in the blink of an eye. It had been nearly forty years earlier that I had gone to Cardiff to study English, French and Italian. That had been in 1965, the seminary was 1994. Cardiff had been Beowulf and Bunyan, Baudelaire and Pirandello, now it was Theology, and Counselling. Now I did Clinical Pastoral Education Units on oncology wards of major hospitals. This was *real* life.

There is something sobering in going on a Sunday morning to visit a hospital, an addiction centre, a nursing home as a chaplain and to do a service in each. As part of my training I had to visit all three. Never before had I been so conscious, that indeed for some, my sermon might be the last one they would hear.

Many of the hospital chapel congregation were seriously ill oncology patients. It put a different perspective on things. I tried not to get caught up in my love of study, but to name things as they were.

Fear – the fear, of life's ultimate questions.

That was what people wrestled with – whether in London or Lhokseumawe, Japan or Jeddah.

I grew; I was moved by those I met.

I felt some of the pain of the many AIDS victims, those whose lives were overwhelmed by heroin. I saw the sad loneliness of the families whose loved ones were struck by Alzheimer.

I saw it in their faces and it touched me to the core.

★★★

There was more. In the hearing of the life stories of others, I simultaneously processed my own. In seminary tutorials, I heard my classmates talk about their marriages and relationships. They were nothing like mine. I heard people share their joys and sorrows.

It was ironic that as part of training, and later, I was chaplain to a Divorced and Separated group. That 'D' word had not really come into focus for me.

The affair in Belgium was a long time ago, forgiven and put behind us. We had a family, I had my studies, I was busy and after all, Michael was forever travelling. I was going for ordination – divorce was far from my thoughts. The Divorced and Separated Group had, however, a tremendous impact on me. I saw lives restored.

The group was held at a church. It was not a religious group as such but was viewed as an outreach function for the community. It was run along the lines of AA.

There were five minutes or so, allocated at the beginning, for each person to say what they needed.

John, a plumber, had been the *dumpee* as opposed to the *dumper,* left with two daughters, eleven and thirteen, when his wife had gone off with her lover.

Her leaving note had made him feel his life was over.

For the first five weeks in the group, he could not say a word, the tears just rolled down his cheeks. Over the next months, John gained confidence. He took a cookery course; he set up a network of friends. He asked women from the group, to support and organize those 'girls days' when he needed help with his growing teenage daughters.

Some five years later, I was chaplain again to the group. John had got his life in hand; he had moved on and was happy. I have never seen such an adored father.

Then there were the odd stories that were told at the group. There was Greg, who wasn't sure if he had really been legally married at Las Vegas. He had been in an alcohol-fuelled state after a binge. He was, he thought, a groom. Greg had slipped through the weeding and screening net of the Las Vegas Elvis Chapel, now he reckoned he needed to get Separated and Divorced!

★★★

My times back at Princeton were good times, happy times. Happy times as a student – and as a chaplain. The challenges of academia invigorated me. One's working life can be stressed and unhappy. Mine has been a joyful wonderful adventure, a mixture of the tragic and the comic.

I mentioned the hospital – Robert Wood Johnson Hospital in New Brunswick. I completed two units of Clinical Pastoral Education there. I was trained to be 'a non-anxious presence in the face of crisis.' I trained on the oncology wards. I lived the codes, the defibrillations. I heard the sound of the helicopter landing on the roof of the building. "Code Blue" and I ran outside from the ward with its cancer patients, to see the medics and technicians rush to save a dying arrival lowered on a stretcher.

Then there were the car crash victims, the failed suicides, the 'chemo' patients, the women who had lost their hair, who so often looked like the mothers – and not the wives – of the men who visited them. Life in all its tragic fullness was in this place.

I thought of the lift men of David Evans, Swansea, of Mr Jordane, I yearned for the fashion floor and the nifty shoplifters who would unscrew a clock before my eyes and walk out. They had no place here.

This was life in all its fullness and all its rawness.

This was my time sitting beside the beds of the dying; being with the families in Intensive Care, standing by the doctors when they gave the news that nothing could be done.

★★★

And yet… my times at the hospitals were greatly enriched by the privilege of knowing and enjoying, the life that was Pearl Rosenblatt.

It was Princeton Hospital.

For twelve years, she had fiercely battled the cancer that she was told would kill her in one.

Pearl had spent more time on the oncology ward than off it. She had been through more operations than the young surgeons who performed them. She was a fighter. The regular hospital chaplain was on break so I took over some of the patients.

"Would you like a cup of tea or coffee? Have you had lunch? If not, we can get you a pizza."

I did a double take. This was a hospital room, wasn't it or had I strayed into the staff room? No it was truly the abode of Pearl. The hospital became her place of hospitality she brought joy, love and homeliness into that hospital ward. Pearl considered herself the hostess. A host who offered a guest, tea, coffee – or a slice of pizza!

Pearl, had been brought up an orthodox Jew. Early on in her illness she had, after one of her many operations, shared a double room. That night, she had experienced something, or as she herself would tell you, *someone*. It started as a bright light. She would tell the story the same each time. She *knew* who it was. Forthright 'say it as it is Pearl' – spoke to the glaring light before her.

"I am not praying to you!"

A particular Nazarene carpenter was the very last person an orthodox Pearl Rosenblatt expected to meet. Especially not in the shared double room of a Princeton Hospital.

But meet him she did.

It was one of the arguments that, uncharacteristically, Pearl was destined to lose. The next day she announced to her shocked family that she was 'converting' Convert she did, not just a little but totally – lock, stock and barrel.

To say she 'had witnessed' to those entering her hospital room doesn't even cover it. Visiting nurses, family, and consultants came out not only with a smile, but with a text.

When Pearl in her quiet moments of suffering, spoke to me of her faith; the light shining this time was inside her. She knew what suffering was big time, but her inner spirit was totally uncrushed, she knew God. She loved life.

The chaplain on duty one day had been alerted that a patient was lying on the grass outside and it was feared that someone, had, in desperation, fallen or jumped out of an upstairs window. It was Pearl. It was Pearl soaking up the sun on what she felt to be a glorious, God-given day.

"Can you bring me in a box of drinking straws?" she asked me one day.

"Of course," I said, realizing how even the smallest action of drinking fluids might be difficult for her. I didn't give it another thought.

The next week a group of representatives from a major drug company, together with Pearl's surgeons and consultants were to visit her – she was taking part in ground-breaking clinical trials for a certain drug.

No one had any illusion as to the seriousness of Pearl's condition. She was a woman who had survived multiple major surgeries and according to the book should have long ago joined the Heavenly Club.

Solemnly, they knocked and entered her room. She was propped up in her bed.

On her head were attached two enormous cardboard mouse ears and on each side of her mouth were taped giant whiskers.

Propped up in bed before her shocked audience, she looked, from one to another, and said seriously,

"Gentlemen, I believe that the mouse extract compound in the drug trials is having serious side effects."

The mystery of why Pearl needed the straws was solved.

When Pearl died, a plaque was put in her honour on the ward. It had been her wish to be buried as a Christian with the cross engraved on her coffin. That was not to be. Instead, I wore the cross on my liturgical stole and shared the funeral with the Rabbi chosen by Walter, her beloved husband.

Her son did not attend. The money he had been given the day before for a new suit for the funeral, had bought his cocaine.

★★★

My visits to the nursing home were a delight. One of the oldest residents, a man of one hundred and five, was the oldest decorated Jewish veteran in the U.S. Amazingly he tried to sort me out on my Hebrew studies. By the time I did my visiting rounds, he was always up and dressed. I still was in awe that as a young man in Russia he had actually seen the Czar.

This was the place of stories and memories.

Another time I was walking along the corridor when I passed an elderly woman standing there, fully dressed. I asked her why she was there.

"I am waiting for the Trenton bus," she said, "it will be along any minute."

Thinking this was my great opportunity for dialogue, I stood next to her. After a few seconds she said, "What are you doing?"

"I am waiting for the Trenton bus," was my answer.

"Are you mad?" she responded, "there are no buses in here!"

***

There is something else about elderly women that can be equally disarming. The young male doctor and I entered the room. She was in her eighties, she sat in her chair.

"Doctor," she said, "I think you need to examine me."

She started unbuttoning her blouse. In that moment I felt I was in a sizzling X rated movie. There was no mistaking that the libido of an eighty-three year old does not diminish with the ageing of the body.

Life blooms eternal!

***

Soon my studying, my times of chaplaincy were complete. My theological years of hospital, nursing home, counselling and Hebrew were ended. I graduated. Many of my courses had beside them a straight A.

It felt good.

After three full time years I had a Master's Degree in Divinity; the graduation ceremony was at Princeton University Chapel. I had jumped all the ordination hoops and committees and I was ordained a few weeks later, I was now The *Reverend* Judith Thomas, Pastor to Reaville Church, New Jersey.

My family were there at the graduation, a proud Michael was there, Queen Bee was there, another milestone.

Reaville – had a Presbyterian Church. It was a historic white 'picture postcard' type of church. In the hallway, we had a telegram from President Reagan displayed. In the year seventeen hundred something, Whitefield had preached in the field nearby to a congregation of over three thousand.

That I should ever have a congregation like that – was in my dreams!

The church had been on the main stagecoach route from Philadelphia to New York. Reaville had spawned other churches, but this church, which in its heyday had seen seventy children in the Sunday school, had seen its peak.

Now it was at the crossroads of its life.

There were houses around it costing a million, a million and a half dollars, alongside the farms. There were those whose families had been baptized in that church for generations, there were those who had no church background, but who wanted their children to have a religious education.

In a Sunday service, there would be Irvin (who wanted prayers, because Monday he was driving out of state to Washington) sitting next to John, the Pan Am pilot (who wanted prayers because Tuesday he was dropping food relief to Somalia)!!

Warren owned the land near to the church and at meetings I knew, that when Warren looked downwards, I was in for trouble. His wife Ethel looked like a character from the Flight of the 'Valkyries,' pigtails on top of her head.

Jack, Warren's brother had on one occasion stayed behind in church after what I thought was quite a punchy sermon I had given.

He sat at the back, head in hands. 'Moved in the Spirit', I thought. I sat alongside him in the pew and he said.

"Something terrible has happened here today."

Conviction of sin came to mind in the matter of George Whitefield or a Wesley. Maybe the sermon I preached had been better than I thought,

"Can we talk about it?" I asked in my most pious tone,

"Look," he replied. It was indeed a sight. Dirty long – johns showed beneath the enormous split in his trousers which went from one knee right around to the other. It was that split, rather than the moving of the Spirit in all its fullness, which had kept him behind when others had left the service.

Who says God hasn't got a sense of humour!

It was in Reaville Presbyterian church that I also got attached to the Word of God in a special way. Warren had painted the pulpit with a cheap varnish, not seeing the need to tell anybody.

When 'Thomas the Church' leant just a bit too forward in the velvet trimmed black Genevan style preaching gown, 'Thomas the Church' got stuck. It was some weeks before my vestment came back duly repaired with a new black velvet panel.

While at Reaville, I used my days off to study for another theological degree, again at Princeton. This time it was the Master of Theology, the Th.M. which could only be completed after one had the Master of Divinity. It took me two years and a thesis. Study was a joy for me, not a chore to be avoided.

Michael was still travelling, the children went to bed early and instead of sitting before the T.V., I studied.

I wrote about church conflict, I read about pastoral counselling with women, I learned of dealing with the depressed and the addicted. It was a time when I realized that there were marriages where love between spouses abounded and overflowed, that there were marriages that were supportive. It was a time that showed me what was missing in mine.

It made me think about what I was going to do, when the three children grew up and went away.

QUESTIONS:

Have you had to cope with a major illness?

What has been your experience of people, who like Pearl, make use of humour to cope with the tragedy in their lives?

The author writes of a long held desire to study and to be ordained. What is it in your life that still remains to be achieved?

There seems to be a tangible sense for her that a life milestone has been reached. What are the milestones in your life?

Chapter Sixteen

JAPAN REVISITED

Now ordained, now with a parish, and the children well past puberty, life was going ahead – but the marriage situation remained the same.

Then news came of another assignment, but this time with a difference.

The next assignment would be a year in Tokyo in preparation for the longer project in the Middle East.

The Japan part meant that Michael would be doing considerably less travelling. Somewhere, deep within, unconsciously perhaps, I felt that this was last chance territory for our relationship. This was a move which would result in the family being together.

Go for it, take the new assignment.

It will be one year in beloved Japan again and then probably three years in Doha, Qatar in the Arabian Gulf.

The children were excited. I have been the constant Welsh cheerleader in the family. There in body, cheering them on prior to every move, whipping up enthusiasm, preparing the goodbyes.

It came as a moving statement, when, years later, Alison in her essay for her Ivy League University at Brown, Rhode Island;

was asked if her parents' mobility had been an inconvenience in her life. How did she feel about it all?

She wrote that it was 'one of the blessings of her life.'

Now adults, all three children speak of the wonderful opportunities that seeing the world in this way gave them. Owen would go on to study international politics in Pittsburgh; Jess would work for a company with links in various countries. All three know the bigger picture.

★★★

Here we were, back to Japan. Back, to Tokyo. The first time I was in Japan, I would keep a book in which I would write the number of women I saw in '*kimonos.*' Now, Japan had moved on and so had I. We were all modernized. I renewed my acquaintance of Professor Iwanaga. I still prepared the detailed questions.

No longer was I a teacher at '*Mussashi No Joshi Daigaku.*' Now, as an ordained minister, I helped at Tokyo Union Church. I preached, and I celebrated communion. I was the Spiritual Director of the church's Women's Society which numbered over five hundred. I wrote and spoke at retreats and seminars.

However, my time and lessons with Iwanaga San – my Japanese professor student – of twenty years previously, were sacrosanct. He would elucidate as before on the intricacies of ancient political situations.

His study was crammed from top to bottom with books. I cast my mind back to all those years before, when at the break in our lesson, he would gently tap the shoji rice paper wall, and Mrs Professor Iwanaga would appear. She would appear in dark kimono, *'chikatabi'* socks. She would have come in almost bent double, so as not to stand higher than him. She would, with the grace of a Madame Butterfly, put down on the low table before us, two cakes.

The cakes had been wonderfully different each time.

Gracefully, silently, delicately, she would back out without turning her back on him. We would then continue with the fascinating unravelling of world politics through a Middle Eastern viewpoint. I learned all about the Ottoman Empire, about the Balfour partition and a hundred other facts.

Now, sitting in that familiar room, we were twenty five years later. He knocks the *shoji* rice paper wall. I wait for the expected pause and the cakes. He tapped the *shoji* again.

Nothing.

He tapped again and then an ethereal, disembodied voice comes from the other side. It was 'Mrs Professor Iwanaga.' My grasp of Japanese enabled me to understand the words, "You'll have to wait, or get it yourself. I am busy."

Hallelujah for the advances in the situation of women throughout the world!

★★★

This time being in Tokyo was different. It was strange to have a Japanese daughter who did not fit the Japanese mould. She spoke hardly any words of the language. When people would start a conversation with her, she would reply in English, "I don't speak Japanese. Ask my mother."

147

I, who had struggled hard – all those years before – with the alphabets – *Kanji, Katakana* and *Hiragana* – I would rack my brain for an appropriate response. It was a place to reflect again. The children were growing up, they would soon be graduating. It would be Michael and I in an empty nest. We would then face his retirement at some point, we would grow old together. Was this what I wanted? Did I want to spend the rest of my life in what would continue to be a monologue?

I did not know the answer, but perhaps underneath I did, and was afraid to verbalize it. Still, I had other things to think about. We still had the next assignment coming up – the Middle East.

I was looking forward to the excitement of yet another new culture.

QUESTIONS:

How is it for you when you revisit a place many years later?

The author writes that Alison was 'out of place' culturally because of her ethnicity. She was Japanese but could not speak the language.

Have there been times in your life when you have felt 'out of place?'

Mrs Iwanaga in the chapter seemed a product of the increasing independence of women. What have been some examples from your own experience of a changing culture for women?

Chapter Seventeen

DOHA AND THE COMPOUNDS

We arrive in Doha, at two in the morning, on the day that Princess Diana died.

It was to be the desert experience in more ways than one. Doha is in the Arabian Gulf, a little bump. It was 1997. We had not been able to get much information at all as to what we could expect in our assignment. Certainly no one had been able to tell us what happened as regards to practicing one's faith. There were certainly no churches visible, quite the contrary; Qatar was next in Islamic strictness to Saudi.

I was apprehensive but confident that I would be able to do *something,* even if it was to study yet another Theology course by correspondence.

We were taken to our compound, a large house with marble everywhere. Unable to sleep, the children had put on the television and it was then, we heard the news that the HRH, Diana the Princess of Wales had been killed in a car accident.

It was one of the times that you are aware that you are far from home, not part of a group experience.

We were of course expats, *expatriates*, out of our country.

151

My children were 'third culture children,' whose parents were of a different culture, born abroad, and they were living in a third culture. Years later I was to lecture on just such issues at Sussex University.

★★★

To arrive in a foreign place, not knowing anyone and to be prepared again for the busy round of getting installed was always a stimulating challenge to me. Maybe hearing of this tragic early death of Diana now jolted me, reminded me once again of where my life was going. Life, I knew from my hospital days was fragile indeed, often cut short when one least expected it.

In the weeks that followed – the children, happy at the American School of Doha, father visiting the refinery daily – I involved myself in the usual activities. I also felt this time that somehow the assignment of three years plus was to be a profoundly fruitful one, fertile ground in the desert. Just exactly how would it work out?

We were soon to discover that religious services *were* held. There was an Anglican service held in the gymnasium of the British School. The priest, Ian, who was also Archdeacon of the Diocese, worked there as a teacher as well as being a cultural attaché.

This afforded the vital diplomatic immunity.

We were, after all, in precarious territory to be openly practicing the Christian faith. Proselytizing was completely forbidden. The service was for non-Muslims. I was to be involved in this Anglican service on a weekly basis, I was ordained and had parish experience. Services were held on Sunday evenings. They were also held on Friday mornings because this was the weekly holiday in Qatar. On Friday, men would attend the mosque.

I held Bible Studies at home, helped with pastoral and counselling matters. Above all, I ministered to women.

Like any new place we had the joys and frustrations of settling in. My first week in Doha had been an example. I, who am not wild about driving anyway, *had* to learn to drive if I was going to do things like get to that Anglican service.

There is something special about having a strong enough motivation to do those things we fear. For me, getting to services far outweighed the trepidation I would feel each time I drove to a roundabout. Driving in Doha was something else, the biggest car wins, you race to one of the junctions and then you take your life in your hands. Mercifully, if the car is a large, four-by-four Toyota Prado, you have a better chance. Each time was a mini miracle and adventure for me.

★★★

Then there was *that* time in the Prado.

I was with Carol from the Bronx, who had never, ever been outside the good old, U. S. of A.

We were off on a simple expedition downtown and to a coffee. We had arrived at the shopping area, parking was a snitch, or so I thought.

I started to reverse into the parking spot and 'Biff.' The noise outside caused an immediate, deep sinking feeling in my stomach. I get out and there *it* is, there *he* is. *It* was the brand

153

new, sparkling white BMW with a huge, scratched, horrible dent on its front side, and beside it stood a local Qatari in a spotless white garment the '*thobe*.'

'This is it,' said my soul, 'Carol and I will never be seen again' She has mentally said goodbye to the good old U. S. of A. Carol is crying, I am past frantic, I am totally off the scale of being 'a non-anxious presence in the face of crisis.'

"I will pay, I will pay," I start to chant with depressing urgency and resignation, thinking that this means a life of endless servitude in some Bedouin tent. I look at him.

He is stunningly handsome. *Really* handsome, if it is possible to be frantic and to think simultaneously – that a life of servitude in the desert with him – might not be such a bad idea, I did!

Then, in wonderful Oxford English, with a smile that melted Carole and I on the spot, he looked at the two heaps of humanity before him. Turning to me, he said, "It is more than you can afford. Do not give it another thought."

How can anyone not love Doha after that? How could I not jump to the defence of Gulf Arabs? I was a convert. Sheiks, Emirs, Tuareg Tribesmen – my knight in shining *thobe* had coloured my view forever.

★★★

This was a country of such contrasts, The culture of the country where women would be totally veiled, where women in coffee shops would lift up their veils and amazingly sip their drinks underneath It was a country where wedding receptions would be 'women only' and 'men only' affairs.

154

I had been invited to one such wedding reception with three other Western women. One of the young Qatari men in our husbands' office was getting married. The husbands all went off to their function at one hotel, leaving by seven o'clock that evening. We, ladies, went off to our venue at another.

What to wear had been a difficult choice. We eventually all chose long black dresses, high necks, long sleeves, and some very subdued jewellery. We arrived at the hotel ballroom and seemed to be about the only ones there.

We waited, we waited, and we nibbled some hors d'oeuvres. Two and a half hours later, just a few more veiled women had dribbled in. We decided we had had enough. As we made our bid for freedom, a large veiled black mass blocked our way and signalled us all to sit down again. We did.

Soon a swarm of veiled figures entered, about two hundred of them. Simultaneously food appeared – mounds of it.

Plates were grabbed and enormous piles of every kind of delicacy placed upon them. We were slow off the mark on this competition and in comparison looked as if we were on some semi-starvation diet. It all happened so quickly. So fervent was the grabbing of the food with hands, some of us was wishing we had brought plastic raincoats.

Finally, with our pathetically small mounds of food, we four sat down. We sat at a large round table with about twelve other women. Food was devoured in minutes, and then whatever the signal was, we missed it. Yet, at one moment, it all changed. Veils and coverings were thrown off and we were sitting at a table with twelve women wearing designer, vivid-coloured sequined gowns with plunge necklines, no backs, low backs, slit to the waist gowns, and provocative, sexy, leave-nothing-to-the-imagination gowns!

We four, on the other hand, looked like Puritans. Every one of the final three hundred guests seemed to be similarly dressed.

The women's orchestra of about ten women started playing and literally letting their hair down. They stood and swayed swirling their waist long hair to the Arab music. All the harem movies I had ever seen seemed to come to life. This was *real* belly dancing.

We definitely looked and felt like Puritans.

It all lasted about another half an hour, then again, by some signal which we obviously missed, again, the veils and coverings were put back on in one black *Tsunami* wave across the ballroom floor.

We saw two men enter. It was the groom and his father, the bride, (we think it was the bride), again veiled, left. That seemed to be the end of it all. Party time was over.

When, we got back home all our husbands were already fast asleep. Their event had lasted only about two hours, and all they had done was put up a tent! Oh the joys of different cultural experiences.

★★★

Doha was very special to me. To walk along the *Corniche*, the promenade, with its bluer than blue Arabian sea alongside, to pass the veiled black outlines that jogged. They were unidentifiable as human, apart from the white sneakers which showed beneath periodically.

It was conservative and quaint. I had long adapted now to the driving, we had been on excursions to the dunes, and we had weekly barbecues with the many South African families there.

The weather was wonderful. I am always cold. Now I was perfect. I loved the tee shirt which had on its front the words, 'The Warmest Summer I Ever Spent Was a winter in Doha.' Here, where you could literally fry an egg on the car, my faulty, internal thermostat was at peace.

I was contented.

★★★

I started to think about what I could do to maximize what would be my three years there. I had my two degrees in Theology from Princeton, my Master of Divinity and my Master of Theology. I had always been passionately interested in ministry with women, women's groups, women's Bible studies, women's this, women's that, after all, I was at a distinct advantage, I was one!

I decided therefore that I would go for the big one. I would apply for a Doctorate.

I would write about this desert experience and I would focus on women living on compounds in the Middle East. The compounds were all over Doha, some of nearly a thousand houses, others smaller. In addition, I lived in one. Ours was a compound of eighty houses, a cluster of expats of different nationalities.

I had lived in similar situations in other places, such as in Indonesia, in Lhokseumawe. I knew what it was like first hand, this life in a goldfish bowl. It had been my experience for much of the thirty plus years.

Life in the gated, patrolled, expat blocks. Yes, 'life in the goldfish bowl' would be my theme, my area of research. I knew it intricately. I would interview women; I would fine-tune it to the Middle East. I would write about how hard for an expat I knew it to be – out of one's country and away from family and friends.

I would write about the three cultures of the Compound, the Company and the Host Country.

I would focus on the pastoral care, how difficult it was to live within the three cultures. I would relate it to other Desert experiences, the Desert Fathers and Desert Mothers. I would write about the stresses such situations fostered, the marriage break ups, the teenage rebellions, and the alcoholism. I would look at it from so many different angles.

My mind raced, I was fired up. I would write to universities and apply to do a Doctorate. The next weeks saw me frantically writing off. Finally, after much negotiation and letter writing, I was accepted by San Francisco Theological Seminary.

Perfect. I saw that my training and passionate love of study, of Theology, could give even the smallest nudge forward, the little bit of help to someone else in their life journey.

I felt I could say and write something that might help these women find their desert assignments meaningful.

Like, most things in life, I did not have it *all* planned. Like those other times in my life – the 'White Mack' devastation of Belgium, or the discovery of my adoption, something else came, 'out of left field,' as they say in baseball.

★★★

In this happy life of Anglican services at the school, women's groups, where I was the perfect corporate wife, amid the walks along the Corniche, amid children and their friends; Wham Bam, Alacazam, *it* happened.

A major incident, a *really* major incident, a capital letters event, *IT* happened.

It was a Friday. Friday, as I mentioned earlier, was a Sunday to all intents and purposes. A service was held at the British School. I was preaching that day so we took two cars and went there independently. I realized I had forgotten something.

Michael and the family had left in the other car, and I returned quickly home to get what I had left behind. I rushed upstairs, picked up what I had forgotten and just as I turned to leave, I saw a piece of paper left by the bedside table. It was not mine. It was in Michael's handwriting. I looked at it and read:

"I will try and phone tomorrow. I think about our time together. I cannot get you out of my mind…"

He was in the habit of making notes prior to important business calls. I soon realised that it was not one of those!

How I got to church and preached I do not quite know. I know that my colleague, Ian, asked me if I was O.K. he thought I looked a 'bit odd.'

That evening I carried out the interrogation. I am something of an expert in this field. My kids, after all, would tell me not to interview people at the bus stop! I suppose it was easier for Michael to confess than it was to avoid the questions which came at him like rapid machine gun fire. In a nutshell, when I thought he was in Singapore on business, he was in Thailand with a woman.

I never, never in a million years contemplated such a thing. Here we were thirty years later! The 'White Mack' devastation had long been put to rest and we had chugged along. It had never occurred to me, not in my wildest imaginings, that he would risk all, risk his marriage again.

This was different from all those years before in Belgium. He knew, I knew, there would be no going back. Now all these years later I had the green light to end it all. Hallelujah.

All the components of my earlier story, all the tears, interwoven with deep reflection over the years, brought me to this final liberating decision.

★★★

Later that day Michael saw my clergy colleague, Ian. They talked. I spoke to my Bishop, but I was in some mysterious peace. I told Michael, I would stay until the children were sorted out university-wise, I would stay then – divorce. Looking back, it was not hard. Ours was not a close knit relationship.

If I needed a "biblical" reason, this was it.

I had trekked to the other end of the country to see him at Lancaster University when he was a student, I would spend hours in the train to get there, only to sit and wait, in that joyless library while he tries to solve his mathematical puzzle. Some warning bell should have rung in my Welsh head then.

So it came as a shock, now in Doha that there really was another person with whom I was living, about whom I knew very little. So now, with great relief, my decision had been made to end to end my marriage.

"He snores," I say to the children, as I choose to sleep on the enormous landing in our marble-floored Doha home. It is almost as large as a room.

We continued to attend the company project evenings, we entertained. I only shared what had happened with three, trusted people. I knew I would need emotional support these next months. Others never knew, never guessed. It was so civilized, no rows, no emotion. I was still the mother, he was still the father.

Whether he thought that I would change my mind, I don't know. We continued in the marriage and the blip of it on the marriage life support machine, that would eventually move to that long, silent line…

★★★

My thesis, however, took on a new passion. I interviewed women. I knew deep down, first hand, I could recognize those marriages that were a sham. I saw in their faces some of the emptiness inside. Each interview with them threw light on my own situation.

I would write about the culture of the multinationals. It was 'the company' as the addictive substance. I knew what was involved in the ethos of the multinational, where the men travelled on business from one country to another.

I knew first hand that they would be exposed to all that the big wide world, downtown 'Ginza,' and Singapore's 'Bugis Street,' could throw at them.

They would be exposed to it, but they also need not let it destroy marital trust and the sanctity of all that meant for the family. I had known from these expat women and others what a one-night stand in such places could do to their marriages, many were destroyed.

Later in Oxford, I would hear other Theses about human trafficking, women bought and sold. Surely, women were of more value than this? It reminded me of the Korean 'comfort' women I had interviewed in Tokyo. Now elderly, they knew only too well what it was like to be treated as a commodity.

I would write about this company culture and also the third culture – that of the compound where women feared to share their feelings with other women. Husbands worked in the same office, one person's husband could be the other person's boss. I would write about all this.

Yes, I would use the wisdom of the past, the Desert Fathers, St. John of the Cross, and the eighth century pilgrims of the Egyptian desert. These ancient voices would have something of value to help those for whom life outside Dallas, or Torrance refinery was just a soul-deadening experience.

Write I did. It was catharsis, it was satisfying.

★★★

Three years later, it is 2000. I am still in Doha.

The girls were in university in America; Owen had his final years in High school. Enough was enough. I felt that for all our sakes, I should return to the USA, to Princeton and our house and that Owen should come with me.

I had planned to stay in the marriage, to stay in Doha, until Owen would leave for university. I couldn't. I was tired of sleeping on the landing I was tired of the monologue. I was a strong woman, but not that strong. I would return to the U.S and start the divorce.

I left and started the proceedings. It took two years.

QUESTIONS:

There are some humorous moments as the author describes this tragedy.

How does humour help you in such moments?

How do you feel the author should have dealt with this second betrayal?

What would have made you stay in such a situation?

Or would you leave?

Carrying on some kind of normality in difficult situations can be overwhelming. What has been your experience of this?

Chapter Eighteen

GIVING UP THE GREEN CARD

How do we cope with things? We all have a coping mechanism, which can let us down or immediately spring into action. When Michael had an affair in the first five years of marriage with my so-called best friend, I lost weight, was devastated but marched on.

In counselling women since, I know that one such event does not necessarily mean the end of a marriage. Confidence and trust are strained to the utmost by such a betrayal, but it need not end the relationship. Marriages can not only survive through this but can also go on to become much stronger.

I had stayed; I had put it behind me those years before. Our marriage, however, had atrophied. The disconnection that had been there, at the outset, got wider. Now in this event almost thirty years later, how different I felt. No devastation, I got on my knees and thought, "Now I have the reason to leave." It was a liberating moment, and far from the old hurting ache of rejection.

No regrets. That's what I told him. That is how I still feel. No regrets.

★★★

Now, it is Princeton again. I am back in America; it is two years since I had left Doha. The girls were in University, Alison in Brown, Rhode Island, and Jessica in Oberlin, Ohio. Owen was graduating from High School and preparing to go to Pittsburgh University. No regrets for any of it. Not for a moment. It has made me who I am. To have stayed would have destroyed my spirit.

We were a family, but we are a different kind of family now. That was what I told him as we sat in the motel. That is what I reflected on as I sat in front of Michael.

★★★

It had been an interesting few days to say the least. The previous day, we had come before a New Jersey judge in the company of our lawyers. In the face of the three inch documented file prepared by my attorney – Michael, had agreed to finalize and to close the chapter. He had dragged it out for two years. He had not sent documents when required, he had lost papers, and he had 'forgotten' information. Eventually, he cooperated. The three inch file was convincing.

The judge commended both of us on how we had dealt with the matters. She had commended us on the fact that we had ended a long term marriage of thirty two years without rancour. Thirty two years of marriage ended with a court pronouncement and an embossed gold sticker. Ours was, at the end, a civilized divorce, lacking negative emotions and acrimony.

Thirty two years of marriage were dissolved legally there and then. This was now a very different, family of five. The children loved their father and he loved them.

We left the Courthouse and immediately went to Owens's graduation from High School, from our divorce to the High School graduation of our son in the same day!

How ironic that the timings should have occurred as they did, but we had no choice in the court scheduling. Sometimes events in our lives are far outside our wishes and desires.

We were the epitome of the decently divorced couple with the photographs to prove it. We were proud parents, clapping as we, and his sisters, watched him receive his High School Diploma. In the evening we went as a family – mother, father and three children – to the restaurant to celebrate. To celebrate what – the divorce or the graduation – I am not sure.

"I have no regrets," I told him and I sincerely meant it.

I had three wonderful children and a life experience of the world which was second to none. I had achieved a lot. All in all, everything weighed up – no regrets. I had done the crying, years before, I had prayed the prayers into the ground, I had screamed at the betrayal during my McVities Digestive, Spaghetti Bolognese Belgian months. I had done with it.

We had both benefited. His had been a supportive, move anywhere/anytime wife and his career had soared to the advantage of all of us. He had provided for his family and had loved his children. We had both changed from our first meeting of organizing social events for B.P. industrial students.

We had grown up.

★★★

I had gone to his room in the motel, where he was staying, to collect some final divorce papers. The cleaner saw me as we came out. Michael and I walked together to breakfast. He tucked in voraciously to his bacon, eggs and whopper waffle.

I sat opposite, the tears streamed down my face. The wedding ring was no longer on my finger. All the memories of the assignments, the adoption, the births, the sadness all hit.

It was sad, the end of a marriage.

"I would like more toast," he said to the waitress, who I instantly recognized, as also the cleaner from moments before.

A few seconds later, she threw 'Frisbee-like,' the toast at his plate. She slopped the coffee refill in his cup. For her, the sight before her eyes was the same old familiar story.

I could hear the words buzzing around in her head, her headlines – 'Married Man Finishes with Mistress' – the bastard! He is telling her over breakfast in a bloody motel restaurant. No wonder she is bloody crying her eyes out, the rotten swine."

She had seen us come out of the room, she had seen such couples many times before, no ring, the affair over and she added two and two and made five. How different from the truth was the scene before her.

He never understood why the breakfast service was so appalling and I never told him.

★★★

I reflected later that all my married life he had referred to 'Queen Bee,' my mother as 'Mrs Davies.'

"Thank you, God, that the green light has flashed big time in this joyless, sexless, lonely marriage," I say inwardly. I smile when the Oscar nominations are called on television. I deserved one, for all those 'O Worship the Project Nights,' for all the three times a week black tie functions, for all the corporate dinner parties. No one guesses. Yes, I deserved an Oscar. Yet, as I had said earlier – there were no regrets.

We had been victims of our time. Naïve. We had seen the world. We had experienced the various cultures; we had brought up three wonderful children whom we both loved. He had been a good father. I had not been beaten (as my father had mentioned on my wedding day) we had developed, grown, we had matured and now we would go our separate ways.

I had no regrets. Neither, I think, did he. What I would have regretted, was *staying*.

★★★

Years later, when Alison would marry her beloved Geni, Michael and I sat next to each other (her wish and ours) at the high table. We walked into the room together, as parents of the bride.

In his speech as father of the bride, he would talk lovingly of our wonderful daughter and the miracle of her adoption. There we were proud, loving parents, relating to our children in our very different ways. We had spent thirty two years together in the journey of life.

Forgiveness takes many forms. It takes time. It takes work. I could not preach nor counsel anyone if I held in my heart the devastation of a 'White Mack Moment' or 'the Singapore Sling,' it all seems so very far away now. Not forgotten but past memories that cause just a twinge of sadness, and the occasional tears as I look at old photographs of the five of us.

All gone, all put away. That wonderful phrase – put down to 'a life experience.'

QUESTIONS:

The author writes of very emotional and poignant moments.

The discovery, the betrayal, and the end of their marriage.

She also later writes, "No regrets." She writes it many times. Do you feel that can be possible in such circumstances?

What does it mean to forgive? Do we have to forget?

How does divorce affect children?

What has been your experience of divorce, perhaps personally, or in the life of someone you know?

What was your reaction when you read that the author, and her former husband, was able to sit side by side at their daughter's wedding?

Chapter Nineteen

OXFORD SPIRES

"How would you feel, if Mother leaves and returns to live in England?" I asked the three offspring separately, and together. There were no objections.

I thought and mulled it all over for months. After all, I am exotically Welsh, a thorough European with a penchant for the good old Church of England. I think about it all, pray and take advice. On the advice of clergy colleagues, I apply and go to Cuddesdon Theological College, Oxford. I attend as the Rev. Dr. D. Judith Thomas.

My Doctorate was titled – "Guidelines to the Pastoral Care, of Expatriate Women Living on Compounds, in the Middle East." This had been awarded to me in 2002, by San Francisco Theological Seminary.

The house in Princeton is up for sale, Alison is in process of completing her time at Ivy League Brown University, and Jess finishes at Oberlin University, Ohio. Owen is now in Pittsburgh, studying International Politics at the University.

The time seems once again right. My three all give their unqualified go ahead. With two suitcases, (the rest of everything in storage) I embark on another adventure.

★★★

Coming back to the Church of England, to the Diocese of Oxford meant that I had to be updated, double-dipped in the ways of Anglicanism, after a minor grazing outside the fold. I had to be made kosher.

Here I was, at age fifty five; years after my 1965-1968 Honours English degree, at Cardiff, here I was being a fulltime, residential student again, living in a small college room, sharing a bathroom and toilet, with at least six others.

It was worlds away from compounds and the corporate life – but it was an adventure. I did not miss Princeton or the five bed roomed house. I was enjoying another new chapter in Cuddesdon, which had turned out more bishops in the C. of E. than many other colleges.

Cuddesdon had been situated outside Oxford so that its students would not be contaminated by the influence of the nearby city. 'Contaminated,' we didn't need to be, we had our own licensed bar in the college.

I was the second oldest student. It was a carefree time studying about the joys of the Reformation, looking forward to the monthly skits called 'Happy Hour' where, with a wonderful irreverence, we were the equivalent of Oxford's Footlights. It was glorious. If I had to wrestle with the bureaucracy of the Church of England so be it. I had been ordained seventeen years earlier but if this was the way it had to be done, 'double-dipped,' as it were – so be it.

It was a glorious "Brideshead" time. The children visited, Mother visited.

All was well with the world.

★★★

I left Cuddesdon with a Diploma for Theology Graduates, awarded with Merit. It was a delight. Now my details were circulated and I would be once again in parish life. I had requested a 'House for Duty' position. The last thing I wanted was a parish of my own; been there, done that.

I was to receive an invitation to an interview and weeks later, it was life in a vicarage – a House for Duty priest in a parish between Reading and Maidenhead.

Yet there was sadness. I missed looking out from the pulpit and seeing a whole range of skin colours and national dress. The 'Lord this' and 'Lady that' did not make up for the cultural mix I had grown to love.

It was not the Britain with which I had grown up, not the Britain where children were seen and not heard, where there was an intrinsic neighbourliness, certainly in Wales.

This was the Britain of heavy immigration, asylum seekers, begging on the streets, binge drinking and drug addiction.

My academic withdrawal was staved off by hooking up with a group of anthropologists in Oxford and once a week, I would go back there to attend lectures at Queen Elizabeth House. This was again a putting of pieces in the jigsaw.

What I had gleaned from my travels was now defined in a statistical way, the social trends, which had resulted in this, or that situation, defined. I was able to see a pattern. It was the coming full circle, which is why of course I needed to be shaken up, yet again. I had still travelled; the position gave me that flexibility.

I had visited the kids, gone on holidays with them, and been to Vietnam to spend time with my brother and my sister-in-law.

Did I want a full time parish? No I didn't. I wanted to travel and to minister in the bigger picture. Four years later, I made the decision to retire. I would do it in June.

I retired on February 18th 2007 and a wonderful caring, loving parish gave me a cheque for almost twelve hundred pounds and I bought the proverbial laptop to write everything down.

I said, I retired yet more was to happen.

The December before that February, after the Christmas services, I had gone to Doha, to visit friends.

"You have come to help us," they said. Ian, the Archdeacon, was retiring from Qatar.

"No, I just came for a late December, New Year break."

I have felt on more than one occasion a dig in the shoulder from above. Two days after I had 'retired' I flew to Doha and took the congregation through their Lent and Easter services. I even had HRH Prince Charles and HRH the Duchess of Cornwall in my first service, they were on a private visit to the Gulf.

The timing in my life has always been "*kairos,*" God's time, as opposed to clock time. I feel now it is *me* time.

I feel it is the time to write. To write for me to understand better the turnings and paths I have taken, to appreciate all the good from these thirty two years of marriage.

It is to write so as to resonate with the joys and pains of other women, maybe to help them focus, put into perspective those most complicated two words – their lives.

QUESTIONS:

The author asks her children their views on her possible return to England.

What do you think you would have said if you had been in their place?

How do you think you would have adjusted living in one room and sharing bathroom facilities after having enjoyed the luxury of a large house and benefits of a corporate lifestyle?

How do you react to the prospect of moving house, maybe of moving countries?

Chapter Twenty

THE PASSING OF 'QUEEN BEE'

I think back to my doctoral thesis. My doctoral thesis had made use of William Bridges' book, "Transitions" and its three aspects – the endings, then the fallow, neutral zone so essential to a new beginning and then finally, the move forward, the new beginning itself.

Nothing in our lives is ever wasted.

I would go through those empty painful moments again, willingly, if they bring me to the point in the spiral where I am now. My relationship with my children has filled me with increasing joy and admiration for what is involved in parenthood. I never thought that I would experience adoption or childbirth.

I have had children who mercifully have never given me in their adolescences, many of the heart breaking problems that parents so often have.

Alison went to an Ivy League college; the baby with sticking up hair is doing research into schizophrenia with Suffolk University, Boston; studying for her doctorate in Clinical Psychology. She is a married to Geni, an Albanian musician. He specializes in *shakuhachi,* the Japanese flute. I am a very proud mother and mother-in-law.

Jessica took herself to San Francisco and to my amazement and great pride, got herself an apartment and a job, working for a major downtown IT company, plus in the meantime she is getting lots of stock options. She is wonderfully creative with a great zest for life. Mr Right will have a treasure.

Owen, whom I still refer to as 'Baby Boy', went back to college to get his MBA at Pittsburgh and is starting a new career. Baby Boy has flown the nest and is now tentatively eating some vegetables and fruits. Sue, his lovely and wonderfully supportive girlfriend, succeeded in steering him in this direction, where I had failed. Well done. It is moving to see someone mature into manhood, into a fine young man.

Michael and I are so proud of all three. This was something we did well. Parenthood with its fumblings and faults came out right in the end.

Now they have to complete their own complicated immigration papers!

***

I do not get academic withdrawal symptoms, I have it under control. I get a shot in the arm attending the anthropology lectures in Oxford. Aged, blue stockings yet mixed with the dynamism of discussing rights for women.

I recently read a book by Ayaan Hirsi Ali "Infidel" about her life in Somalia. It reinforces to me that "yes" there is something to be learned in these events, the fun and the tragic. It is the daring to be exposed and vulnerable.

I think of those influential books I had read so many years ago at Princeton. Nelle Morton writes of "bringing our stories to speech." At college, I took an autobiography course, and as part of it – we were told to get into a group – and for as long as it took and without interruption, we were to tell our stories. We were all so very different, and it brought out tears. It was holy ground, not that it was tragic, although some parts were, it was holy because someone listened to who we were, what made us tick.

★★★

Now it is full circle. I think of the women who have influenced my journey, as I hope, I have influenced others and will continue to do so.

Seeing my mother in the nursing home, for me, brings it full circle; together with thinking about the people of my youth. I look at her and all these memories merge, the cultures mingle, women all over the world, snapshots, vignettes. Memories and thoughts, both happy and sad.

Past and present all fuse together.

How on earth did my grandmother manage to peel onions without a single tear, to clean brass or silver without a single black mark on her hand? I remember people of my childhood, of the past. I remember Alice, my grandmother's friend, who wore about seven layers of clothes. Alice was raped at sixteen by a local farmer and forced to put the baby up for adoption.

Now I appreciate the sadness of it all.

It was a preparation for the counselling of women that I have enjoyed all over the world. All these stories fuse together.

There was Mary, our childhood neighbour, who, when I came home from school would be sitting in our kitchen, having a cup of tea with my mother.

Poor Mary, her over-permed hair was like coarse wire, but she always had the knack of giving you just the right present for your birthday or Christmas. Her lot was enduring mental cruelty. Peter, her husband, behind closed doors did not speak to her for weeks on end, but out in public would be the attentive husband. Coming, as she did, from a large and loving family, this was punishment indeed, a burden she could hardly bear.

They died within six months of one another.

***

All these memories merge with the 'Sitis,' 'Sudars,' 'Tomokos,' 'Mrs Iwanaga's' of my life. I think back to other marriage relationships, attitudes to ethnic diversity, and continents away from my own.

One of the very few times that I saw my mother, Queen Bee, lost for words was when we went to Oxford Street to see the Christmas lights. We were at one of the underground stations.

There was a porter from Jamaica. At age eight, I don't think I had actually ever seen a black man. I had heard about coloured people and took that to mean they might be blue or pink.

She asks about the next train. Not oblivious to her Welsh accent, he then said, "You are not from this country are you?"

Words failed her.

Then not wanting to stop there he went on, "Don't they have trains in your country?'

My racial tolerance was born that day.

Memories, memories. It reminded me of how my father had said of eight-day old Alison, of her Japanese ethnicity, "Don't worry she will grow out of it!" It is that song from South Pacific, "We have to be carefully taught, to hate and to love." All this conditioned me for my roving life and travels.

I never heard my father speak badly about the Germans even though he had fought them on the beaches of Anzio, Monte Casino, or in North Africa. He did not talk of his war experiences.

All that my mother said was that when he returned home after the war ended, he stopped going to church.

All those events are now in the past. It is all part of listening to, dealing with, and learning from, the stories of others.

★★★

Perhaps the most momentous passing was that of Queen Bee, woman extraordinaire. She was regal even in death.

She, who had been a role model, she who had set my feet on the path of decency, She, who, when I returned to England – would ring me every day, as I often do to my three children. She has impacted on all aspects of this exotically Welsh life.

Technically, she did not give life to me, but as I had done with Alison, my mother had taken me and nurtured me. She adopted me, as I had later adopted.

"I am now ready to go in somewhere," my mother declared one day, during one of my visits. I heard and I knew I must obey. I knew that she had given it all the most careful thought. I drove down from Oxford not long after and I moved my mother into the vacant room at Brombil Nursing home, just across the road from where she lived.

She would reside, no, she would *preside* there.

I would travel down from the Vicarage and we would dine at the Castle hotel in Neath. It always amazed me to read that Lord Nelson had stayed there. I hope he had found it in a better condition, than when my mother and I would visit.

We would eat our predictable lunch there. Two breaded plaice, to be followed by an ice cream with chocolate sauce (for her). En route, pushed in her wheelchair, she would often give unsuspecting passers by an almighty push. She would make comments, as to this or that one's, external appearance, often exclaiming in a loud voice, "Look at the size of her!"

Queen Bee held court in Brombil Nursing Home.

If she had been born in a different generation she would have run a country. Now, with her walking stick taken away, (she has been too active prodding other residents awake), she sits in full majesty. Hair done once a week, nails varnished and jewellery adorned.

"I am dressed up, why aren't you?" is the comment I receive as I arrive on my monthly leisure advance – pensioner train ticket from Twyford to Neath.

Queen Bee was a 'Brombil Escapee' extraordinaire. In the early days, she had observed the security code punched in by the staff as they go off shift. This 'Nonagenarian Houdini' would then fly the nest, coat on and going at break-neck speed up to the town. As she walked out with an unsuspecting visitor, she would comment, "It is so nice, isn't it, to visit these old people!"

It was my mother who, by osmosis, has given me the spunk to see me through crises, forever reminding me that I am a member of the Warrior Race.

I have needed to know that so much over the years.

My mother was jealous; dominant, forceful, and extremely capable. She was a force to be reckoned with, reigning as 'Brombil Queen Bee.' I telephoned one evening, it was late – ten o'clock. I wanted to tell the staff at Brombil that I will be taking the train from Oxford the next day, getting there at one o'clock to take my mother out to lunch.

The phone clicks.

"Brombil Nursing Home."

I recognize instantly the disembodied voice at the other end.

"Mam, is that you?" I am in shock. I continue, "Mam, what are you doing?"

The reply comes as if it was the most natural answer in the world.

"I am just helping out. They are useless here!"

She has been my role model but also perhaps a reason why I was unprepared for my marriage and stayed. I had not only my birth details hidden, but a part of me which I have now discovered.

Recently someone sent me some number of facts in an email. It mentioned major inventions all by women – the bullet proof vest, the laser printer, etc. Feisty Queen Bee could have invented something given the opportunity.

Feisty Queen Bee, who nursed my father at home in his last throes of cancer rather than let him go into the hospital, a place he feared and dreaded.

Years later I asked if her she ever had misgivings about my marriage to Michael.

"Yes, I did"

"Why didn't you tell me?"

"You would not have listened."

I, who was a hundred per cent compliant, I don't think so. I would have heard her words as if from on high.

Now it is all a long time ago.

On one of my visits, she gives me "the look." This time my intuition was on high alert. This time I go down to Wales again the following week, something I never did, visiting in two consecutive times. I plan to stay.

I stay the night in her room and… I say goodbye.

I anoint her and I am "Judith the Priest." I say my goodbyes. I say all that I ever wanted to say to this forceful woman who had shaped me. It is farewell. She drifts out of consciousness. I feel it is complete.

Two days later, I am on the ferry to Santander, Spain, and I get the expected news from the nursing home. Queen Bee has died. December 17th 2010, A few weeks later, on January 1st, she would have been ninety nine. She died a week before the anniversary of my father's death, twenty years before on Christmas Eve. Christmas services are special to me.

I fly back from Spain and share the funeral service with her local rector. It is I who has written and will deliver the Eulogy.

It is the full circle; her life and death encompass my ministry to women. Hearing their pains and joys, enduring some of their struggles, experiencing how mothers mould their children in unseen ways, both good and bad.

This is a chapter closed. It is also another chapter opened. It is all part of my life as a woman.

QUESTIONS:

What do you feel has been the author's relationship with her mother? How would you describe it?

What has been your relationship with your mother? How has it differed from your relationship with your father?

If you are a parent, how has your relationship been with your children?

How do you feel about the decision of placing an elderly parent in a nursing home?

Is it one that you have made, or may have to make in the near future?

Chapter Twenty One

FINDING MY SPORTY SELF

These last few years I have travelled to many new destinations, places not previously visited. I have *developed*; I proudly tell my incredulous friends on the telephone, I have *discovered* my new "sporty self." There is always hesitancy on the line in response to this and I hear the words, "It is a bad line, could you say that again."

To go up on a ski lift, or to go in a gondola without feeling that I am going to die any moment, has given me a sense of achievement at least equal to that of receiving a degree – if not more so.

Walking on what seemed to be the knife-edge of Machu Picchu in the Andes, or to be in a perilously open Zodiac boat watching icebergs fall into the sea, has opened up new 'vistas' for me.

Why now, after years of hesitating to swim without my feet touching the bottom, why now, was I qualifying to be a 'one-star kayaker' on the river Thames?

What brought the change?

The answer is not a *"what"* but a *"who"*. This has been affected by a person – Ron. It has been my marvellous, wonderful Ron, that has brought me a new dimension –

but that is another book. He is the person who shares my life, who has enabled me to know the depths and joys of married life as it should be. That is my husband Ron.

I know also that the two inches of plastic (white around the collar) has added something to his life.

When the Welsh whirlwind – whirled into his life, something changed for him. We have even visited Patagonia together and met Welsh-speaking South Americans. Now, many years and many events later in my wonderful second marriage, I have discovered love.

This is no matrimony monologue in this marriage. This is sharing, compromising, discussing, enjoying, experiencing, driving mad, forgiving and being forgiven, writ large.

I can understand better what is meant by the 'holiness' of it all amid the very real physicality. It is *'Collar to Cleavage.'* Cleavage as a metaphor for all that it means to embrace my womanhood, my sense of being feminine, of being capable and a voice 'brought to speech.' To understand in the later chapters of one's life what is meant by, 'the spark' is a blessing indeed.

★★★

A few months ago I gave a seminar for thirty women entitled, "How to Swim in the Goldfish Bowl of Life Without Drowning." I looked out at the women before me, some known to me. Some had cried about their lives. The husbands of two of them had committed suicide in the most tragic of circumstances.

During the last three hours of the seminar, I play the song, "It's Raining Men, Alleluia," and they laugh.

190

I stand there, at the seminar, no clerical collar, no scripture references, no talk of *lectio divina,* no Desert Fathers.

They are not ready yet.

They have yet to discover the spiritual. It is a chapter, a stopping point. *'Collar to Cleavage.'*

It is time.

A few weeks earlier I had gone through the routine to renew my clerical licence. I am now able to officiate at services again, whenever I am in England. My life, like all our lives, has certain Ecclesiastes timing.

One woman comes up to me after the seminar. "I wish someone had said all that to me twenty years ago." Perhaps there's a part of me that echoes that sentiment. Another woman comes up and cannot speak through the tears. We meet two days later and I hear her story. Years earlier, Princeton days, I read the book, "Women's Ways of Knowing." We all have our stories to share.

Back home, after a Sunday service, I take off my collar and pull on my sweater over my new, wonderful push-up bra. My clerical shirt and my collar of two inches of white plastic are on the dressing table. I go forth. The collar will still be there when I get back. Whether I wear it or not, I *know* who I am. I can concentrate on counselling. I can write. I can spend my life with wonderful, supportive, love of my life, Ron.

I think of those places yet to be visited, other chapters yet to be written. Who could have regrets? Not me.

"How great, how great is our God!"

Amen indeed.

QUESTIONS:

In answer to the question, Where are you now in your life?
What would you answer?

Where have you resonated with the author's life experiences?

What issues has the book raised for you?

It seems that the author has managed to resolve, forgive and make sense of what has happened to her over the years, there has been healing.
Has this been the case in your life?

If you were to write your life story, what would be the title of your book?

ACKNOWLEDGEMENTS

My first acknowledgement is to my husband Ron, for the hours spent editing, reading, re-reading the manuscript and offering suggestions. He is always 'there for me.' I am truly blessed.

There are many people mentioned in the chapters to whom I owe a great debt. They intersected my life, some leaving an indelible mark. Others not mentioned in the book have touched my life in a deep way. They will not all be named here. The list would be impossible.

My three children, Alison, Jessica and Owen have shaped my life in their very different ways. They are my three joys. I am immensely proud of them.

My brother Martyn, his wife, Lynne and my niece, Emma represent the influence of my Wales heritage.

My friends, Sandra Fouracre and Sheila Burgess have been my supportive friends for over forty years, together with a school friend, Michael Davies.

When I first lived in Princeton, Dorothy (Dotty) Samms influenced my faith in the deepest way.

I give my thanks over the years, for the friendship of Ed and Debbie Gwazda. Also to Laura and Mitch Lison, all have been wonderfully supportive. Sheila Bowes and her husband, Emmerson, by his financial advice, have kept me on the straight and narrow for many years.

Ursula Burnett, the godmother to my beloved Alison, a great friend and a role model for a strong woman.

My spiritual life has been influenced beyond measure, by Michael and Rosemary Bent, Clive and Jane Handford. Clive was my Bishop in the Middle East.

My Bible study friends – Ranee Savundranayagam and Jan Wiersma – have been a great source of influence and strength to me. My friend Laura May has been my prayer warrior over the years, as has Gay Hundley. Debbie Davis of Princeton Seminary, my former tutor, is my mentor and friend. Together with Carol Saysette of San Francisco.

There are many whose general kindness has brightened my life, Teresa and Alan Davies, Valerie Charlton and Jo Wilson, Janette Davies, Helen Beard, Heather and James Brennan. Recently Fr. Jeremy Harris, and those in the Wednesday congregation.

Some of my friends and influencers are no longer alive to read what they meant to me – they include, Ben and Tricia Broerse, Alan and Mary Mason; all in my thoughts.

Finally, I would not be the person I am today were it not for 'Queen Bee,' my father and a loved grandmother, Gramma Davies.

A big 'thank you' to all for what you gave to me.